99 TIPS FOR CREATING SIMPLE AND SUSTAINABLE
EDUCATIONAL VIDEOS

99 TIPS FOR CREATING SIMPLE AND SUSTAINABLE EDUCATIONAL VIDEOS

A Guide for Online Teachers and Flipped Classes

Karen Costa

Foreword by Michelle Pacansky-Brock

Sty/us

STERLING, VIRGINIA

COPYRIGHT © 2020 BY STYLUS PUBLISHING, LLC.

Published by Stylus Publishing, LLC.
22883 Quicksilver Drive
Sterling, Virginia 20166-2019

Library of Congress Cataloging-in-Publication Data

Names: Costa, Karen, author. Title: 99 tips for creating simple and sustainable educational videos : a guide for online teachers and flipped classes / Karen Costa; foreword by Michelle Pacansky-Brock. Other titles: Ninety-nine tips for creating simple and sustainable educational videos
Description: First edition. | Sterling, Virginia : Stylus Publishing, 2020. | Includes bibliographical references and index.
Identifiers: LCCN 2020007707 | ISBN 9781642670851 (paperback) | ISBN 9781642670844 (hardcover) | ISBN 9781642670868 (pdf) | ISBN 9781642670875 (ebook)
Subjects: LCSH: Video tapes in education--Handbooks manuals, etc. | Interactive videos--Handbooks, manuals, etc. | Web-based instruction--Handbooks, manuals, etc.
Classification: LCC LB1044.75 .C67 2020 | DDC 371.33/5--dc23
LC record available at https://lccn.loc.gov/2020007707

13-digit ISBN: 978-1-64267-084-4 (cloth)
13-digit ISBN: 978-1-64267-085-1 (paperback)
13-digit ISBN: 978-1-64267-086-8 (library networkable e-edition)
13-digit ISBN: 978-1-64267-087-5 (consumer e-edition)

Printed in the United States of America

All first editions printed on acid-free paper
that meets the American National Standards Institute
Z39-48 Standard.

Bulk Purchases

Quantity discounts are available for use in workshops and for staff development.

Call 1-800-232-0223

First Edition, 2020

For Andrew and Fred

CONTENTS

FIGURES

Supplementary videos are provided to correspond with certain tips. A playlist of all videos can be found by scanning your smartphone camera over the QR code in Figure F.1.

Figure F.1. Playlist of videos throughout *99 Tips for Creating Simple and Sustainable Educational Videos.*

Note. Retrieved from https://www.youtube.com/playlist?list=PLp1oNaMlolJNcLBT440n-R-4B_meQG4Ic

QR codes linking to individual videos can be found in:

FOREWORD

Not long ago, recording a video required specialized tools and skills and often meant hiring an expert. As a result of advancements in digital technologies, this is no longer the case. If you have a computer with a webcam or a smartphone connected to the Internet, you have what you need to record and share your own videos and make some life-changing shifts in your teaching and your students' learning.

For educators, the video revolution is especially important. Technology has transformed the teaching and learning landscape by providing students with more opportunities to learn at a distance. Fully online and blended courses have increased access to higher education for more students than ever, which is especially important for students from minoritized groups who are less likely to have the privilege of being on campus full-time. Amid all of this change, there is one constant: A supportive student-instructor relationship is the key to meaningful learning. A 2014 report by Gallup and Purdue University based on a survey of 32,000 college graduates concluded that undergraduate students with a professor who cared about them as people, made them excited about learning, and encouraged them to pursue their goals and dreams were more likely to be highly engaged in the workplace and report a positive sense of well-being. Technology will continue to reshape our educational landscape, but quality human interactions will always be key to a meaningful life.

And that is precisely why this book is so valuable for you. Each time you teach a course, you have the opportunity to change lives. If you are teaching online or blended courses, the time your students spend engaging with your online course content is an opportunity for you to untangle a sticky concept, quickly review last week's lesson, share a supportive message before an exam, or take students into the field to a relevant destination. Mastering the skills to record simple, brief, and authentic videos for your students will enrich their learning with your human presence.

Karen Costa has developed a practical resource that will answer all the questions you have about video but are too afraid to ask or perhaps simply don't know whom or how to ask. The bite-sized tips in each section will guide you through a scaffolded journey to develop the digital fluencies

needed to seamlessly use video to interact with your students. You will discover the theoretical background about why video is important in teaching
and learning and be introduced to oodles of witty strategies that will help
you find an approach that works best for you and saves you tons of time. And,
perhaps the best part of this book is that the author will be with you every
step of the way. Keep your smartphone handy and scan the QR codes (the
funny-looking, pixelated, black-and-white squares) with your smartphone or
a QR-reader app, and the author will appear before your eyes with a warm,
friendly message for you.

Using simple and sustainable videos in your teaching will help you establish trust with more of your students and convey to them that you care about
their learning. When you begin implementing the tips in this book, you will
notice more of your students leaning in and working harder so they don't
let you down. And you know what? You'll be reenergized and love your job
more than ever before. This book just may be the most transformative teaching resource you've ever had. Enjoy the ride!

Michelle Pacansky-Brock, EdD

Reference

Gallup. (2014). *Gallup-Purdue index report*. Retrieved from https://news.gallup
.com/reports/197141/gallup-purdue-index-report-2014.aspx

INTRODUCTION

99 Tips for Creating Simple and Sustainable Educational Videos: A Guide for Online Teachers and Flipped Classes is intended to support educators in creating videos for their students and to empower online educators to make use of their videos to humanize the online learning experience. You'll notice an emphasis throughout the book on simplicity and sustainability—in other words, offering an approach that requires little in the way of technology, that can be implemented quickly and easily so that you feel encouraged to use it often, and indeed reuse what you've created in subsequent courses—saving you time—while providing guidance on developing videos that reinforce learning and pedagogical goals.

In addition, land-based teachers who wish to make better use of the flipped classroom model (Tucker, 2012) will also benefit from this book.

In my higher education work over the past 15 years, faculty have consistently reported to me that they've felt scared to create a video and pressured to make a Hollywood-style production. Some offerings on video development for faculty include trainings in multiple educational technology platforms that require extensive video editing and regular maintenance of expensive software. While I'm sure there's an audience for this, many faculty just want to create simple videos to connect with their students. Due to time constraints and busy schedules, faculty also want a video development process that is attainable and sustainable. Instructor-created videos should be part of our teaching toolboxes, but current training and advice around how to use videos often ignores the needs and challenges of both teachers and students. This book offers a new path forward that aims to not only inform but also inspire

This book offers today's educators simple strategies that you can begin using in less than an hour. These strategies are built to last; they are not huge time drains, and you can easily replicate them from term to term. In many cases, the videos that you'll create using this system will eventually begin to save you time as you become a more efficient and effective instructor through the use of engaging educational videos. Here are all the ideas and guidance you need to begin the transformational journey to creating and sharing videos with your students.

The Online Education Landscape

More than six million students enrolled in at least one online course in 2016, according to a recent Babson Survey Research Group report (Radicioni, 2018). In the words of one of the study's coauthors, Julia Seaman, "The growth of distance enrollments has been relentless" (Radicioni, 2018, para. 3) While overall higher education enrollment fell in 2017, the percentage of students taking online courses grew. Online education is poised to become the new normal in the next decade, pointing to the need for quality resources to support online faculty in their journey toward teaching excellence.

With growth comes a combination of challenge and opportunity. Research on online education has shown a wide variety of outcomes, from no significant difference (Russell, 2001) between online learning and traditional learning, to mixed results (Jones & Long, 2013), to better outcomes in land-based courses (Xu & Jaggars, 2013). Online education and research into its outcomes continue to motivate educators to mitigate challenges and develop strategies to increase its efficacy.

Despite the somewhat muddy findings on learning outcomes in online learning as compared to traditional models, research is clear (Dixson, 2010) that when online learning is at its best, it's because of a strong online professor who develops engaging and motivational relationships with students (Jaggars & Xu, 2016). In short, helping faculty to build regular, positive, and interactive relationships with students is the key to a successful online learning experience. Teaching matters. In an online course, it appears to be even more critical to student success than in a traditional classroom setting. Instructor-created videos are a tool to develop and cultivate positive teacher–student relationships. The teachers and institutions that prioritize those relationships, I believe, will lead the way into a new era of higher education that truly lives up to its name.

Flipping Out

I pay close attention to first lines in novels. Here's one of my favorites, from author Meg Wolitzer (2008) in *The Ten-Year Nap*: "All around the country, the women were waking up" (p. 1). All around the world of education, it seems to me that the educators are also waking up. We are waking up to the value of active learning and intentional pedagogy. No longer are we satisfied with being the sage on the stage, lecturing at a class of passive students. Our time is too limited, and the stakes are too high.

Some of you are coming to this book because you wish to flip a land-based classroom. For those new to flipping, it's the process of shifting the dynamic in a classroom. What we traditionally do during class time is instead done for homework, and class time is used for interactive activities and practical application of course concepts. In many cases, teachers create video lectures for students to view at home before class within the flipped model.

There are many gifts and challenges to flipping your class, but one of the potential obstacles to making this shift is a hesitation to create instructional videos. In addition to helping online educators use videos in their courses, this book is also for the flippers out there. Your desire to create more active learning experiences in your classroom is admirable, and your fears about videos are human. This book will help you grab onto your humanity and turn it from a hindrance into an asset.

My Video Creation Journey

As a high school junior, I chose to take an elective media course taught by my favorite English teacher, Mrs. Bestwick. In this extremely hands-on class, we hosted a morning television show, "The Morning Minute," that was broadcast on TVs in all of the school's classrooms. If it sounds like a fun class, it was. I also happened to be taking it with two of my best friends. There was a small amount of high school level antics (intentionally trying to make the other person laugh while we were on-air was a favorite), but we also learned a ton. There was something intoxicating about being on camera and knowing that if I had enough "pop" in my presentation, I could capture viewers' attention, even on the small scale of my high school teachers and peers. By the time I started looking at colleges, I had decided on my future major: broadcast journalism. I would draw people's attention to topics that mattered.

I was 17 years old when I started at Syracuse University, having been accepted to the Newhouse School of Public Communications. I lasted a single semester in the program, and then I changed my major to undecided (my adviser nearly had a heart attack when I told him this plan) before moving on to my final major in sociology. The reasons for my change of plans are complex, but the short version of why I opted out of my dream is this: I was 17. While I sometimes wish I had stuck to my original plan, in hindsight, I wasn't missing out on my goal completely; I was just modifying it a bit.

Many years later, after starting my career in higher education, I began teaching online. After only a couple of courses, I began to ask around for tips on how I could better connect with my students. I had already been teaching land-based classes for a couple of years and I didn't like how disconnected I felt from my online students; I wanted to mimic the connections I had with students in my traditional courses. Through peer support and attending conferences, it became clear that videos were the best option for me to boost student engagement immediately.

As I began making videos for my online courses, I had so much fun rediscovering the joy of being on camera. I felt myself in a state of flow, where the work ceased to feel like work. I spent hours upon hours creating videos for my students on every topic that I could imagine, experimenting with different software programs and tools.

It took me a couple of years before I made the connection between my love of video development and my first college major. When I reflect on how this all played out, I can't help but feel like everything is meant to be. I know a few people who work in newsrooms, and the pace and schedule are both incredibly intense. I was luckily redirected into my teaching work, but by creating instructional videos (and coaching faculty on the process), I'm still able to access that part of me that enjoys being on camera. Over the past several years, I've become more intentional about combining my past with my present to help faculty create great instructional videos. Capturing people's attention through video is not only an effective instructional strategy but also a heck of a lot of fun.

Glossary of Terms

There's an adage that "words create worlds." Language can be used to enliven, to oppress, to illuminate, and to conceal. There are a couple of important distinctions that I wish to make about some of my word choices in this book.

Traditionally, education that took place in a classroom setting with both teachers and students present in the same space was just referred to as *education*. That was all there was. In the early days of what many of us now call online learning, *distance learning* was a common term to denote the physical distance between the teacher and the learner. I don't use that term in this book, and I'm retiring it from my vocabulary. I have built my entire teaching philosophy around decreasing any felt distance between my students and me. We are anything but distant.

Further, many people now use the term *face-to-face* to describe traditional classroom learning experiences. I don't use that term either, because many online learning classes now make use of synchronous video conferencing tools (e.g., Zoom) where online students and their teachers are absolutely communicating face-to-face.

In this book and my work, I'm currently using the terms *land-based* and *traditional* to denote educational experiences that take place in a classroom setting with both students and teachers physically present. I use the terms *online learning* or *online education* to describe education that takes place via the Internet. I think this distinction matters because it speaks to the reality of the work we do, as well as our aspirations for online education.

Another word choice worth highlighting is the use of *pedagogy*. Many of us who work in education are adopting the term *andragogy*, which is a theory of adult learning. Pedagogy actually means "child-leading," and andragogy means "adult-leading." Some feel that we should only use andragogy to describe our work with adult students.

Malcolm Knowles, who popularized andragogy, acknowledged its limitations and recognized that rather than a dichotomy, the shades of difference between pedagogy and andragogy are meant to be more of a spectrum (Aubrey & Riley, 2016). Depending on one's prior knowledge and motivation, some of the principles of pedagogy might be more appropriate for an adult. For example, many of my online students have never taken a college course. Others are both college students and online-savvy students. Their needs vary.

Relevance, a critical factor in andragogy, might be vital to the success of some children. My 10-year-old son wants to be a sports commentator when he grows up. He's recently started noticing that there are no broadcasting courses in his school and argues that he learns more about his intended career reading *Sports Illustrated*. For kids with clear career goals, we should be more explicit in making connections between school and their future work.

What's most important is that we get to know the needs of the learner and make intentional teaching choices. I choose to use the word *pedagogy* to represent the art and science of teaching as a whole since the term is well-known, and the distinctions between andragogy and pedagogy are false anyway. This choice assumes that we all desire to respect the needs of our diverse learners.

I aim to continue to make thoughtful choices about the words that I use in my work and life. I hope this glossary offers you clarification as well as some food for thought about your educational word choices.

How to Read This Book

In this book, I'm going to help you get ready for your close-up so that you too can create awesome instructional videos. Even better news? These tips are both simple and sustainable. They aren't difficult to master, and they won't take up a ton of your time. I know how busy educators are, and I know that starting the journey of video creation is nerve-wracking for most people. Not to worry: The system outlined in this book is built on the premise that by keeping it simple, you'll feel empowered to step outside of your comfort zone and create a video for your students.

Some of you might wish to poke around the tips, skimming through the table of contents and selecting those that feel most relevant. Others will choose to read the tips in order. The choice is yours. Those who are entirely new to using videos in their teaching would probably benefit most from a more thorough and structured approach. If you're familiar with creating videos, jump around to the tips that you think will be most beneficial.

Short introductions to each section will give you a sense of what's contained in those tips. Those introductions are a great place to start if you aren't sure where to begin. Finally, because we all know that the practical application of new skills is important to the learning process, Section Twelve contains a series of six hands-on exercises for you to put these tips into action.

A note on accessibility: I want to highlight accessibility in this introduction because it's essential to the success of both students and teachers; it's not a footnote in our journey. While the focus of this book is not on accessibility, I will cover it in Section Ten. Additionally, the sources cited in that section will point you to some additional resources on the topic. I encourage you to keep accessibility in mind, remembering that all students have the right to benefit from our videos.

Section Overviews

Section One will make the case for why videos benefit both students and faculty. Too much of our current professional development in the education field focuses only on how improving our teaching will benefit students. This section will speak to how videos will make your life easier and inspire you to be a more engaged teacher.

While there are certainly places for "winging it" in our teaching, most of us understand that setting clear instructional goals is critical to student learning. Section Two will outline what goals inform my use of videos, providing you with examples of goals that you can use as you begin your video creation journey. It includes ample, practical examples for how you might use videos in your classroom.

From those practical tips, in Section Three we will turn to some guiding theories and research. I believe that we need theory to inform our daily teaching choices and lives. In this section, you'll learn about a wide range of theories from a diverse range of fields. For those of you who might need to explain or defend your use of videos, this is a must-read section.

A key assumption of this book is that there's no one-size-fits-all solution to teaching, learning, or videos. In Section Four, I'll help you consider your unique teaching needs and compare and contrast different types of videos. Don't worry though; we'll keep it basic. The options listed are all simple and sustainable.

Once you've narrowed down the types of videos you plan to create, you'll then want to start thinking about when and where you'll share these videos with students. Section Five will offer tips to determine the ideal course timing and placement for your videos. There are pros and cons to each choice, so as you read these tips, know that there's no perfect solution. You can always modify your strategy after evaluating your first attempts at sharing videos.

Some basic preparation leads to high-quality videos. In Section Six, you'll learn how to quickly and easily set the stage for your videos. This section will cover tips about lighting and audio, two of the most common concerns for those new to creating videos.

Many video tips focus too much on technology and not enough on presentation skills, which in my experience are paramount to creating an effective video. The tips in Section Seven probably won't win you an Emmy award, but they will help you be an engaging presenter. Bonus: Most of these tips can be easily translated to land-based teaching or speaking engagements.

Since PowerPoint is a nearly ubiquitous tool in education, I've dedicated an entire section to its use in your videos. PowerPoint is an excellent tool, but it's often misused, to the detriment of student learning. The tips in Section Eight will help you use PowerPoint in such a way that you'll engage students through the most effective design principles possible.

As I've mentioned, creating videos, just like teaching, doesn't have any one-size-fits-all solutions. While many of you will feel comfortable being on camera after reading this book, some of you might find that it's just not your forte. Section Nine will help you make that important decision. Whatever you decide about your on-camera presence, there are tools in this book to help you create high-quality educational videos.

After all of the good work you'll be doing to create videos, it will then be time to share them with your students. Section Ten will offer simple and sustainable strategies for getting your videos in front of your audience in the most efficient way possible. This section also contains tips about making accessible videos that can benefit all of our students, including the use of captions and universal design for learning (UDL).

Ideas and knowledge are great, but in order to enact change, we need to take action. In our busy world, learning how to manage our time and set priorities is critical to our success and to serving the greater good. The tips in Section Eleven will help you move from goal-setting to goal-getting through a series of exercises intended to help you develop your own simple and sustainable video creation plan.

Finally, all great teachers know that practice makes perfect. In Section Twelve, you'll have the opportunity to practice the skills that you've learned throughout this book. Through a series of six practice exercises, you'll overcome any lingering fears about videos and stimulate your creativity.

Viewing Sample Videos

Throughout the book, you'll see QR codes (about one in each section). These QR codes will link you directly to some sample videos on their associated tips. These videos will reinforce concepts from the tips, and they'll give you examples of what a simple and sustainable video looks like.

QR codes in the early days were a bit cumbersome. Not anymore. Simply open your smartphone's camera and hold it over the code. A notification will appear. Click on it and it will take you directly to the video. Let's go ahead and test it out now, shall we? Follow the QR code in Figure I.1 for an introduction video from me.

Figure I.1. Video: *Introduction to* 99 Tips.

Note. Retrieved from https://youtu.be/eUGuqpL8NC4

Now that we've got the big picture, some storytelling, and housekeeping out of the way, it's time to begin your video creation journey.

References

Aubrey, K., & Riley, A. (2016). *Understanding and using educational theories.* Los Angeles, CA: SAGE.

Dixson, M. D. (2010). Creating effective student engagement in online courses: What do students find engaging? *Journal of Scholarship of Teaching and Learning, 10*(2), 1–13.

Jaggars, S. S., & Xu, D. (2016). How do online course design features influence student performance? *Computers & Education, 95*, 270–284.

Jones, S. J., & Long, V. M. (2013). Learning equity between online and on-site mathematics courses. *MERLOT Journal of Online Learning and Teaching, 9*(1), 1–12.

Radicioni, B. (2018). *New study: Distance education up, overall enrollments down.* Retrieved from https://www.babson.edu/about/news-events/babson-announcements/babson-survey-research-group-tracking-distance-education-report/

Russell, T. (2001). *The no significant difference phenomenon: A comparative research annotated bibliography on technology for distance education.* Chicago, IL: IDECC.

Tucker, B. (2012, Winter). The flipped classroom. *Education Next.* Retrieved from https://www.educationnext.org/the-flipped-classroom/

Wolitzer, M. (2008). *The ten-year nap.* New York, NY: Penguin.

Xu, D., & Jaggars, S. S. (2013). Adaptability to online learning: Differences across types of students and academic subject areas. *Community College Research Center, 54*, 1–32. Retrieved from https://ccrc.tc.columbia.edu/media/k2/attachments/adaptability-to-online-learning.pdf

SECTION ONE

WHY VIDEOS WILL WORK FOR YOU AND YOUR STUDENTS

Too many teaching innovations rest on the belief that teachers should sacrifice our well-being for the success of our students. Instead, I argue for a model of teaching and learning that sees the success of faculty and students as interdependent. I want students to succeed. I want faculty to succeed. This book aims to support both of those goals.

Videos are not another teaching tool that will steal your time and increase your stress. By using my simple and sustainable method, you'll create videos that empower you in your teaching, save you time, and help you become a more effective educator, all while helping your students succeed.

The tips in this section will outline the benefits to both faculty and students. You will learn why video is such an effective teaching tool and begin to understand how you can weave videos into your teaching practice without sacrificing an inordinate amount of time or increasing your stress level.

TIP 1: BE PART OF
A MOVEMENT

◄◄ I ►►

When I first started teaching online, I saw online learning as a second-best replacement for land-based learning. I was much more interested in the land-based classes that I was teaching at the time. Today, I am a strong advocate of online learning and the importance of excellence in online teaching. What changed?

First, I started to hear stories from my student advisees about positive experiences in online courses. Students told me that they had struggled with participating in land-based courses for their entire educational lives, only to discover that they finally felt free to shine in the online course setting, released from a great deal of social anxiety. I also worked with students who were serving on active duty in the military all over the world while taking classes online. I met individuals with severe and chronic health issues who would not have been able to pursue an education in the traditional college setting. Online, however, they thrived. In short, I saw the access that online education offered to a diverse population of students.

Second, in February of 2009, I had my first child. By April, I was enrolled in my first online course as a student, pursuing an advanced graduate certificate in educational leadership. I was able to respond to my weekly discussion boards while my son had tummy time on the living room floor. Without this online option, I would've had to delay my education. Knowing how life works, that delay could've been permanent. I also had an extremely positive experience taking online courses, and as an introvert, I felt myself come alive in the learning process as I'd never been able to do in a land-based classroom.

Through listening to students' voices and having my own transformational online education experience, I began to see the power of online education to increase access and success. I found myself speaking out as an advocate for online education, willing to challenge anyone who made blanket statements indicating that online learning was somehow less than its traditional forebearer. I dove into my professional development as an online teacher, learning everything that I could about online pedagogy.

In the past several years, I've come to realize that access is only the most obvious benefit of online education. When done well, online teaching and learning have the power to do things that traditional learning cannot do. Instead of seeing online courses as a second-best option when land-based courses aren't feasible or accessible, what if we become curious about how online education could be even better or could do something new, something special that could fuel a twenty-first-century learning experience?

Because I love online learning, I want to improve it. How can online education be better? The asynchronous nature of most online learning experiences points to some of the possibilities. Personalization of content based on students' unique interests, learning needs (note that needs are different from styles; there's no research to support the concept of learning styles), and ideal learning pace are some promises presented in the online modality. With creative teachers willing to dedicate themselves to learning about and applying innovative solutions grounded in both research and practice, I believe that online education has unlimited potential to help people learn, grow, and contribute.

Access isn't the online promise of online learning; this is a movement. By reading this book, you're taking the first step to contributing to the growth of that movement. Welcome.

TIP 2: RECOGNIZE YOUR POWER

◀◀ ▮ ▶▶

In a recent study of the impact of various online course design factors on student success in online courses, researchers found that while well-organized course design principles are important, the interpersonal relationships between students and faculty are paramount to student success (Jaggars & Xu, 2016). Your ability to form quality relationships with students in the online modality is critical to a student's ability to learn and persist in an online course.

These findings are in alignment with one of the most popular models of online teaching and learning, the community of inquiry (CoI) model. The CoI model (see tip 24) consists of three types of presence: social, teaching, and cognitive (Garrison, Anderson, & Archer, 2000). Social presence, in part, speaks to a teacher's skill in projecting their personality and self through their students' screens. It is often described as "being real" in an online course.

In short, more than content, more than course design, you are the factor in an online course that has the greatest potential to help your students succeed. You have a lot of power. We know that teachers are critical in any educational setting, but I would argue that in an online course, where students are more isolated than in a traditional college or school setting, their instructor is their lifeline, their guide on the path of persistence.

Recognize the power that you have in your online teaching. Step into the gift of developing your social presence in an online classroom and watch your students respond. There is, of course, a great deal that is out of our control when it comes to our students. However, our ability to be real, to be present, and to develop a positive and professional relationship with students in our online courses is a power within our control. Let's begin to recognize, own, and use that power, for our success and the success of our students.

References

Garrison, D. R., Anderson, T., & Archer, W. (2000). Critical inquiry in a text-based environment: Computer conferencing in higher education. *The Internet and Higher Education, 2*(2–3), 87–105.

Jaggars, S. S., & Xu, D. (2016). How do online course design features influence student performance? *Computers & Education, 95*, 270–284.

TIP 3: BUILD RELATIONSHIPS WITH YOUR STUDENTS

◄◄ ▌ ►►

Positive relationships with students have always served as the foundation of my teaching philosophy. While a lot of other factors go into forming how and why I teach (challenge and support, validation, fun, brain-based teaching), all of it rests on my understanding that by getting to know my students, and letting them get to know me, our teaching and learning journey together will be more fruitful and enjoyable.

One of the biggest concerns that I hear from faculty about the challenges of teaching online is that they won't be able to connect with their students in the same way that they do in a land-based setting. This is one of the biggest misconceptions about online education. With some effort, planning, and creativity, we can forge and sustain positive faculty-student relationships in the online setting.

Of course, when we aren't sharing the same physical space with our students, synchronously, two to three times a week, creating relationships takes a bit more effort. Online courses can be isolating if we don't take the challenge of connection seriously. The good news is that developing simple videos to share with your students will support you in that challenge.

A recent study found that when students and teachers discover things that they have in common, students perform better in class. This was especially true for underserved populations (Gehlbach et al., 2016). The relationships that we form with our students aren't just about social interaction; they are paramount to the success of both students and faculty. Videos open up a line of communication in the online modality, allowing teachers to reveal appropriate personal details that can be used to discover commonalities that support our students' academic achievement.

Sometimes, for example, my dog, Rocky, will make a guest appearance in my videos. No longer am I just the professor in the eyes of my students; I am now a dog lover, someone who's a little silly, enough to bring her dog into a video. Being a pet owner is a small detail that I likely have in common with many students in my class. Suddenly, the distance between us, whether it's hundreds or thousands of miles, grows smaller.

How do you approach relationships in your land-based teaching? Your online teaching? How can you foresee using videos to support those relationships?

Reference

Gehlbach, H., Brinkworth, M. E., King, A. M., Hsu, L. M., McIntyre, J., & Rogers, T. (2016). Creating birds of similar feathers: Leveraging similarity to improve teacher–student relationships and academic achievement. *Journal of Educational Psychology*, 108(3), 342–352.

TIP 4: MAKE STUDENTS HAPPY

◄◄ I ►►

I started creating videos for my online courses soon after I began teaching online in 2006. I've taught around 100 courses since then, across a few different institutions. In almost all of those sections, I've used videos as a teaching and engagement tool, but in some classes, due to course content modifications or my busy schedule, I've gone without videos.

I observed two things about these courses without video. The first thing was that they felt different for me. I wasn't as connected to my students. I felt like I was doing a good job as a teacher, but not a great one, and that my course was decent, but could be better. You know that feeling when you put on your favorite pair of jeans versus the ones that aren't quite as comfortable? It was like that—as if my course was missing something.

The second thing I observed about teaching without videos happened in the terms when I once again infused my courses with videos. I not only felt like I was back wearing my favorite pair of jeans but also noticed the number of communications that I received from students. Students e-mailed me about the videos, with no intention other than to thank me for including them in the course. They would post about the videos in the course discussions and mention them in course assignments. Finally, without fail, in each term that I've taught with videos, at least a few students per course will mention the value of those videos in their student evaluations at the end of the term.

What always strikes me about the comments from students about videos is that they are often more focused on a feeling than on the content. Students tell me that they "love" having videos in our course. They share that they are "grateful" for a professor who takes the time to make videos. They've written to me to say that they wish all of their professors would make videos.

There are a lot of compelling reasons why teachers should create videos for their students. One of the main reasons that I make videos is simple: Making my students happy makes me happy.

TIP 5: HAVE FUN

◀◀ ▌ ▶▶

The older I get, the more effort I have to put into making time for fun. While it's a bit of a bummer that fun doesn't flow as naturally for me as it did when I was younger, I also find that because fun is more difficult to come by, I'm much more appreciative of it. Making videos is a lot of fun. That alone, aside from all of the other benefits of creating videos for my students, is worth my time.

When I look back at the videos that I've made over the years, I notice a common theme: I'm happy. I'm smiling, often cracking jokes that make me laugh, and just having an all-around great time with myself and my unseen students. Even though I'm completely alone when making my videos, it's as if my heart and brain are already anticipating the people who will eventually be on the receiving end of my performance. I feel a little bit less alone. My work and life suddenly aren't quite so serious. I am in the present moment and enjoying it.

Sometimes, when I'm in the middle of creating a video, an idea for a story will pop into my mind. I go with it, letting the spontaneous joy of the moment take over. In many instances, I laugh at myself, like when I say, "One last thing," and then think of three more things to tell my students. I'm known to pull a prop from my office space to illustrate points or bring my dog onto my lap (warning: only if you have a lap-sized dog) and introduce him to my students. There are elements of teaching that aren't always that much fun; such is life. Videos, though, are fun antidotes that open up my creativity and sense of play.

I know that many of you might be questioning the potential of this tip because you are nervous about being on camera. That's perfectly understandable. By the time you finish this book, you'll have had a chance to learn and practice the logistical skills that you need to create an awesome instructional video, paving the way for you to get past those fears and hesitations so that you can start rediscovering a sense of play in your teaching.

TIP 6: GET CONNECTED

◀◀ ▮ ▶▶

Online education can be a lonely enterprise for teachers as well as students (I've been both). After many years of working in traditional, land-based roles, I am now a fully remote worker and have been since 2012. Most days, after I drop my son off at school and say goodbye to my spouse, the only living being who I see until school pickup time is my shih tzu, Rocky. He's a great listener, but he's not very effective at offering feedback or verbal encouragement. While I wouldn't change my career choices, loneliness is definitely one of the downsides of remote work.

Creating and sharing videos with my online students decreases my sense of isolation and increases my feelings of connectedness. I feel connected to my students while I'm creating a video, even though I'm alone in my home office. Just calling them to mind while I'm speaking and recording feels like it brings us together in a shared virtual space. After I've shared a video and I receive comments back from my students about how my video has helped them understand course content or to feel less isolated themselves, I'm filled with a feeling of connection.

One of my oft-repeated mantras about online education is that when it's done right, it can be as effective, if not more effective, than traditional education. This argument acknowledges that there's a wrong way to do online teaching and learning. In part, the wrong way fails to address the tendency for isolation in asynchronous, fully online teaching and learning experiences. While I'm sure that some students and teachers can learn, grow, and succeed in isolation, like a lone flower blooming in the desert, for most of us, isolation blocks growth.

The use of videos is one of several antidotes to isolation and one of the most efficient. By creating simple and sustainable videos, you will decrease not only your students' sense of isolation but also your own.

TIP 7: SAVE TIME

◄◄ I ►►

In many conversations about why videos are important in online learning, video advocates talk about the benefits to students. I've also included lots of benefits to students in this book. This is valuable information, but it's incomplete. Videos benefit faculty as well.

Most faculty I know want to create the best possible learning experiences for their students, but they are also very busy. One thing I hear from a lot of faculty is that they will set a goal to use videos in the next term, but that term comes and goes in a flash without any videos. Time gets away from them, and it can seem like more work than it's worth.

That's why I'm here to shout from the rooftops that videos will make your life easier! Let me explain. How many e-mails or phone calls from students do you respond to each term asking you the same questions over and over? Tons, right? I teach first-year students, often in their very first online course. They have a lot of questions, and they need almost constant support. Being a great teacher is time-consuming. What if we could support our students and save ourselves time in the process?

Enter videos. Each week in my online courses, I create an instructional video with an overview of that week's content. I walk students through assignments and expectations. I explain where past students have struggled and how my current students can avoid common pitfalls. I always start and end the videos with a story or positive anecdote. Typically, these videos are 5 to 10 minutes long, and they take me about 15 minutes to create and upload to my course site with zero time needed for editing.

This time is given back to me tenfold in the time that I save from answering countless and repetitive questions term after term. I have taught with and without these videos, and I can attest to the fact that in the terms in which I use videos, I receive far fewer frequently asked question–type queries from my students, and the quality of my students' work is much better. That means I also spend less time working with students on revisions or resubmissions, because they are more likely to get it right the first time. While creating a video might cost you 15 minutes, it will pay you back in saved time.

Later in this book, I'm also going to teach you how to make your videos sustainable so that you can reuse them from term to term. That means that once you invest that 15 minutes in creating the video, you don't have to recreate it. You'll continue to reap the benefits from that video for terms to come, without having to invest any additional time. In short, videos will save you time and make your life easier.

Video tutorials on your course and assignments can be used in both land-based and online courses. If you teach a traditional course, consider creating a video that you can e-mail to students before the course starts, or early in the first week, to help answer common questions.

TIP 8: EXPAND STUDENTS' SELF-EFFICACY

◄◄ I ►►

One of the most insightful quotes that I've ever read about teaching comes from Thomas Carruthers: "A teacher is one who makes himself progressively unnecessary" (Quotes.com, n.d.). This is a necessary reminder that part of our job is to instill a sense of self-efficacy in our students.

Sometimes when a student asks me a question, the most appropriate response is simply to answer them. Other times, when I answer immediately, I'm doing their work for them. Using videos helps me find the perfect balance between supporting my students and challenging them to become self-sufficient.

When I have weekly informational videos available in my course, I can respond to a student's question as in the following:

> That's a great question. Have you viewed the week three video tutorial yet? I believe you'll find the answer to your question there. Check it out and let me know if you still have any questions.

Learning is a partnership between students and teachers. In the preceding example, I am demonstrating this shared responsibility. I am both supporting (by affirming the question and encouraging the student to circle back to me if there are further questions) and challenging the student to utilize the available course resources. In other words, I'm not handing the student the fish; I'm teaching the student to fish.

Consider how you can use videos to expand students' self-efficacy. Whenever you notice yourself working harder for students' success than they are, a video can help shift some responsibility back toward students.

Position your smartphone's camera over Figure 8.1 to view a video about this tip.

Figure 8.1. Video: *Expand Students' Self-Efficacy.*

Note. Retrieved from https://youtu.be/KGN6GVPSp2I

Reference

Quotes.com (n.d.). *Thomas Carruthers*. Retrieved from https://www.quotes.net/quote/11642

TIP 9: INCREASE COMPREHENSION OF COURSE CONCEPTS

◄◄ ❙ ►►

Higher education has a strong emphasis on student learning outcomes, and rightfully so. Great teachers consider what they want their students to know or be able to do as a result of their lessons. Ideally, when our students complete our courses, they have gained a wealth of knowledge and learning strategies that will serve them in their future educations, communities, careers, and personal lives. When our students learn more, they are better for it. This is one of the reasons that I create videos.

Notice that the emphasis in the previous paragraph was on students. What about teachers and faculty? How is facilitating our students' comprehension of course concepts good for us?

When I feel confident that my students are learning, I feel good about myself as a teacher and a person. Doing a good job in our jobs is an integral part of the human experience. Take a minute to consider how you would feel if most of your students failed your course. Now, imagine a scenario where most of your students demonstrated mastery of your course's learning outcomes. How does each situation feel? If you're like me, the former feels quite awful, even demoralizing. The latter fills me with a sense of pride and hope. I want to do good work, and I know that you do, too.

Later in this book, we'll discuss how to create short, instructional videos that demonstrate, emphasize, or explain key course concepts. I call these mini-lectures. This is one of many ways that I use videos in my courses. Rather than solely relying on written explanations, textbooks, or external resources, I find that creating videos about course concepts improves my students' understanding. This benefits students and faculty. These spaces of mutual benefit, I believe, are signposts that can guide us forward in creating a higher education model for the twenty-first century and beyond.

When your students are learning and succeeding as a result of your videos and teaching choices, you will feel more empowered, happier, and more hopeful as a teacher. In addition to helping students, isn't this a great reason to create videos?

SECTION TWO

ALIGNING VIDEO CONTENT
WITH INSTRUCTIONAL GOALS

I n this section, we'll focus on video's role in student learning, but let's not lose sight of the bigger picture: that we are human beings having social experiences in our classrooms and that the success of faculty also matters, along with the success and learning of our students.

You'll learn about my instructional priorities and how I use videos to support them. You'll also explore several ideas around how you might use videos in your courses. I'll mention now, and several times throughout this book, that your video creation process should be unique, born of your personality, teaching style, course's modality, and field of study. Make this your own.

We can be fiercely focused on teaching excellence and student outcomes while also prioritizing our human relationships. This section will show you how to proceed on that path.

TIP 10: DETERMINE YOUR INSTRUCTIONAL GOALS

◄◄ I ►►

Something drew you to this book. Perhaps you have noticed a sense of disengagement and isolation in your online courses, and you want to try something new to add a spark of life to your teaching. Maybe you're interested in flipping your land-based classroom, or a colleague has been using videos in their teaching with great success. Before you get ready for your close-up and push the record button, it's important to take some time to get clear on your big-picture goals for videos. Build on what initially drew you to this book through some additional self-reflection. This is time well spent that will help you avoid getting lost "in the weeds" of your video creation journey.

Here are some questions to consider that will help you clarify your instructional goals:

- In which course or courses will you use video? Many of you teach more than one section and might also teach more than one course. Will you use videos in all of those courses, or will you begin with one?
- What instructional problem do you think you might solve with videos?
- How will your personality influence your video creation plan? Are you very outgoing? Introverted? Are you obsessed with details or more focused on the big picture?
- Who are you at your best as a teacher, and how can videos support those strengths?

There are no right answers here; what's most important is that you get clear about your teaching and your goals. I'm going to share my instructional goals for videos in the next tip. Your goals might be quite different from mine; that's perfectly okay.

Often in the education world, some of our goals come from external sources. If that's the case for you, and you are reading this book to learn about how to create videos because someone told you that you have to make videos, I encourage you to still take this time for self-reflection. Even if this wasn't your idea, I am here to tell you that you and your students can still benefit from videos. Aside from the external demands, take some time to be open to the possibilities that videos offer.

Finally, don't rush this step to jump ahead to the practical details. As a culture, I think we're guilty of belittling the importance of self-reflection. The why of your videos is just as important as the how. The time you spend here, getting clear about what you want from videos, how they will serve you as a person and teacher, and how you envision them supporting student learning, will help you in the long run and make this video creation process more productive and enjoyable.

What are your top three instructional goals for videos? Before you proceed, commit pen to paper (or fingers to keyboard) and write those down. Keep those goals fairly brief and informal right now, because later, in section 11, I'll walk you through a much more detailed process to develop a written plan for video creation.

TIP 11: REVIEW MY EXAMPLE GOALS

Humanity, Instruction, Clarity

◄◄ I ►►

In tip 10, I encouraged you to reflect on, identify, and write down how videos can help you reach your instructional goals. In this tip, I'm going to share my top three video goals with you to give you an example of some elements that you might want to consider. After reviewing my goals, you might want to return to your goals to edit and revise. Goals are meant to be fluid. It feels awful to be working toward a goal that no longer serves us. As you read through this book, return to your goals time and again, revising them as you gain more information about this process.

When I first started creating videos, I had one goal: to overcome frustration. I'd been teaching online for a short amount of time, but I already felt like I was teaching with two hands tied behind my back. In my traditional classrooms, I was able to be animated, to emote, and to engage my students with stories and explanations. Something was missing from my online courses, and I needed to do something about it, for my students and me. Through reading, researching, attending conferences, and learning from colleagues, I identified videos as a tool that could help me instill in my online courses the same energy as my land-based classes.

Many years later, my goals for my videos have evolved as I've developed my knowledge of online pedagogy and as our entire online education community has grown and changed. Today, I have three primary goals for my videos: to humanize, instruct, and clarify. I'll talk more about each of these goals in detail in tips 12, 13, and 14. In short, first, I want my videos to help me appear fully human to my students, rather than seeming like a faceless robot lurking in the shadows. Second, I want my videos to improve my online instruction and help students better master our course learning outcomes. Third, I want to use videos to clarify the logistics and navigation of the online classroom, particularly for students who are new to college or online learning.

Now that you've read my example goals, take a minute to return to your own goals. Compare and contrast. Do your original goals still work for you and your teaching? Are there any elements that I mentioned in this tip that you might wish to add to your goals? Remember, goals are a work in progress. You can revise your goals as you continue to read this book. Further, when you venture forward and start creating videos, you'll learn a great deal from the work itself. There's no substitute for experience.

TIP 12: SHOW YOUR HUMANITY

◄◄ I ►►

In tip 11, I identified my primary goals for creating videos: humanize, instruct, clarify. My first and most important goal is to humanize my online instruction. Let's begin by getting clear about what *humanize* really means.

It's necessary to distinguish between humanizing our teaching and developing our online presence. We talk a lot about presence in online education. You'll learn more about presence in tip 24 when we review the community of inquiry (CoI) theory. Presence lets our students know that we are actively engaged in the online course. I can't say enough about the importance of teaching presence in an online classroom.

Humanizing our online teaching certainly contributes to our teaching presence, but it's a concept in its own right. We could, for example, be extremely present in our online course, regularly logging in, sharing announcements, responding to students' discussion posts, and offering personalized feedback on assignments. We could do all of this, being present in all of these ways, without humanizing our online teaching.

Some concepts are best defined by backing into them, looking at examples before settling on a succinct definition. I humanize my online teaching when I do the following:

- Tell a story about the time that I decided to take tap dancing (my first dance class ever) at the age of 32
- Let students know that while I'm teaching them time management, I'm also still a work in progress who is learning how to manage her time
- Express regret when a student experiences a loss and joy for a big win
- Bring my dog onto my lap when I film a video, introducing him to the class

While these examples certainly show ways that I demonstrate presence in an online course, they have an added layer of showing students my humanity. While most of the preceding (minus the dog introduction) can take place in written form, I find that video is even more useful, showing students my personality, my love of silver jewelry, my predisposition to messy hair, and my growing collection of eyeglasses. To humanize online learning means to show and tell our human stories.

One additional way to conceptualize the process of humanizing our online teaching is to consider the following question: Could a robot do it? In today's world, that's a valid question. Could artificial intelligence have done that work for you? Do your students have confirmation that there's a fellow human being on the other side of the screen? What have you done this week in your online course to show a piece of your humanity to your students?

As mentioned in the introduction to this book, a growing body of evidence points to the importance of the student–teacher relationship to student success in online learning. I believe that humanizing myself through video is one of the most critical elements to building those relationships. Michelle Pacansky-Brock (2017) recommends various types of videos (welcome, feedback, weekly) as examples of ways to develop presence in her model of humanizing online learning, which also includes empathy and awareness.

While I hope this goes without saying, it's best to err on the side of clarity: Humanizing your teaching does not mean oversharing. We can share our human stories and maintain professionalism at all times. I talk quite a bit about my dog, for example, but very little about my son. My students know a lot about my reading habits, but nothing about my personal health.

Think through a few examples of aspects of your life and personality that might humanize your online instruction. If you're stumped here, focus on your field of study. What drew you to this field? What do you love about it? What was your favorite course in college? For some faculty, knowing how to humanize ourselves will come naturally. If not, turn to your wealth of knowledge and passion for your discipline to help you get started.

Position your smartphone's camera over Figure 12.1 to view a video about this tip.

Figure 12.1. Video: *Show Your Humanity.*

Note. Retrieved from https://youtu.be/hyjXXTNl4ME

Reference

Pacansky-Brock, M. (2017). *How to humanize your online class.* Retrieved from https://brocansky.com/wp-content/uploads/2017/09/Humanize-Infog-Letter-Size-for-Printing.pdf

TIP 13: EXPLAIN A CONCEPT

◀◀ ▌ ▶▶

Imagine that you're teaching a land-based course on anatomy and physiology. In today's class, you are starting a module on the human brain. As you review the concepts of neurons and synapses, one of your students raises his hand: "I'm just not understanding how neurotransmitters work, Professor. Can you go over that again?" As you look out over the class, you see several students nodding in agreement. Clearly, you need to take a moment to explain this concept differently and then recheck your students' understanding.

In a traditional classroom setting, we provide that sort of just-in-time feedback to our students by responding to questions and noticing body language that communicates confusion.

Online teaching is different. We need to be more proactive about noticing when students need additional explanations. This is why providing instruction via videos is one of my primary goals in my online classroom.

Information about gaps in students' understanding will come to us in different ways, depending on the activities and assessments we use in our courses. For example, if you make use of weekly quizzes, you can identify which questions were most often missed by students as a way to assess which concepts might need more attention. Discussion responses are another way to check for student understanding. Have you noticed a theme of misunderstanding in students' discussion posts? Receiving lots of e-mails and questions about a particular concept is another indication that your students need more guidance on a topic.

In each of these cases, creating a video is an excellent way to address gaps in understanding and explain a concept in more detail. For example, if students consistently missed question six on this week's quiz, you can create a just-in-time video to address that question and to assist students in understanding the concept.

My sense is that the lack of direct instruction on course concepts based on formative assessments of student learning is an area of opportunity in online teaching. Consider if this could be one of your instructional goals for videos.

For those of you who are land-based teachers, videos might complement your in-class instruction. Have you ever had a student ask a question barely a minute before class ends, maybe even on the last Friday before spring break? Rather than wait until you meet again, create a quick video explanation with answers for students and e-mail it to them later that day, if time allows. Land-based teachers tell me constantly that they have trouble fitting everything into their allotted class time. If that's true for you, consider how videos might help you provide more effective instruction outside the constraints of a 60-minute class period.

TIP 14: CLARIFY A TASK OR NAVIGATION

◀◀ I ▶▶

It's quite typical for me to get e-mails from students asking me how to perform a task such as submitting an assignment in our online course. Students also inquire often about where to find something in the course like the grading rubrics for various projects. In some cases, these are easy questions with quick answers. In other cases, the solutions require multiple steps. When working with new, online students who might not yet be comfortable in the online classroom, responding with written step-by-step instructions can lead to additional confusion. In turn, that confusion can result in a series of back-and-forth e-mails that aren't a very good use of anyone's time.

Enter videos. Why tell them when you can show them? Because I work with first-term learners who are often new to college and the online learning experience, providing clarity is one of my primary instructional goals. Videos support this work.

Once you get to a certain comfort level with video creation, a funny thing will happen—you'll realize that sometimes making a quick video for a student is more efficient than responding in writing. If I'm working with a new student who I know might be baffled by a series of 10 steps to help her get to her desired outcome, I will often record a quick video screencast (see more in tip 40) for her instead. This not only makes the student's life easier and answers her questions but also demonstrates an exceptional level of care. The responses that I receive back from students when I make them personalized videos is what I can only describe as "over the moon." I don't do this all the time, but if the situation warrants it, it's often a good use of my time.

You might also start to notice that several students need support with completing a task or navigating through a particular portion of your course. In that case, consider creating a general video that illustrates the necessary steps. You can then post this in your course for all your students and reuse the video in future terms.

Remember, many of our students are new to online learning and our learning management systems (LMSs). While working in our LMS might be entirely intuitive for us after years of use, try to keep your beginner's mind and remember what it felt like the very first time you viewed your online course. If you're anything like me, it felt a bit like staring into the abyss. Perhaps you also asked yourself, "Where the heck do I start? What if I click the wrong thing and it all explodes?"

Written explanations of online tasks and navigation can work when the list of steps is concise or when we're working with more advanced online learners. When there are several steps, or when your students are new to online learning, consider creating a simple video to help show them how to succeed. Your students will learn more efficiently, and they'll be grateful that you took that extra step to support their success.

TIP 15: TELL A STORY

◀◀ ❙ ▶▶

Now that you have a sense of the top three ways that I use videos to support my instructional goals, the remaining tips in this section will give you additional ideas for how you might use videos in your teaching. These are all practices that I have experimented with over the years. Of course, don't feel like you need to introduce all these approaches into your video creation process. Instead, draw on those that seem most aligned with your own instructional goals.

A few years into my teaching career, I stumbled across a 10-minute YouTube video of college professor Randy Pausch, offering his "last lecture" on *The Oprah Winfrey Show*. Prior to his national television appearance, Pausch was diagnosed with terminal cancer, and he put together a lecture for his students and peers at Carnegie Mellon University. In the lecture, he intertwined stories from his life with lessons that he'd learned about creativity, time management, and living a happy life. It was a hit, finding its way to Winfrey.

I started showing the video clip to my land-based students, and increasingly, I found myself telling more stories in my teaching, inspired by Pausch's approach. At first, I felt like I might be doing something wrong. I had spent a lot of time in academia, so telling stories without offering a full, APA-style citation to back up all my claims felt like I was breaking the rules. Should I really be wasting time telling stories when I could be lecturing about research?

However, along with these doubts and discomfort, I also recognized a shift in the classroom. My students' eyes were more likely to meet mine when I told a story. The energy when I lectured about content was very different from the energy in the classroom when I told a story. I could feel and see an increase in attentiveness and engagement.

Without knowing why stories worked, I was satisfied with my observations that they did. I kept telling stories, and today stories are a huge part of my teaching practice in the online environment, supported by my use of videos. While we can, of course, tell stories in the written form, much like I just did in the previous paragraphs, I also recognize that there is a vast swath of written content in online courses, much more than in a traditional course. Telling stories in my videos mixes up modalities, giving me a tool to connect with my students and to practice creativity in my teaching.

Today, there's a growing body of research recognizing the why behind stories. Paul Zak, for example, is a scientist who studies the neurobiology of narrative. His work explores topics like how oxytocin, a "feel good" chemical, is released when we hear a story. Zak (2015) argues that "narratives that cause us to pay attention and also involve us emotionally are the stories that move us to action" (para. 33). As our understanding of the human brain continues to evolve, researchers are discovering that our brains seem particularly interested in stories—narrative arcs with a beginning, a middle, and an end.

I recently studied the power of storytelling with master teacher and positive psychologist Maria Sirois during a weekend retreat. Sirois had two important recommendations for us in our work as presenters and teachers. First, don't tell a story for story's sake. Make sure your story is relevant to your topic. Second, keep a list of your stories.

Take a moment to jot down a few of your own stories. These don't have to be masterpieces, just simple examples of the human experience. Later, in tip 94, you'll have the chance to tell a story as part of a concluding section of practice exercises. For now, begin by thinking about stories from your life or your teaching career that might connect with your students, moving them to action in their own lives.

Reference

Zak, P. (2015). Why inspiring stories make us react: The neuroscience of narrative. *Cerebrum*, Jan–Feb. Retrieved from https://www.ncbi.nlm.nih.gov/pmc/articles/PMC4445577/

TIP 16: GET THEIR ATTENTION

◀◀ | ▶▶

Attention is a precursor to learning. Here's a simple example. Imagine someone famous whom you admire. Perhaps you follow their work on social media, or you read their book. Place yourself in a room with that person. They're the keynote speaker at a conference, and you're sitting in the audience. As they begin to speak, your phone buzzes. You make a choice in that moment to direct your attention to your phone. You see that you received a text from your best friend who's in a crisis. For the next 30 minutes, your attention is directed at your phone and your friend, not at the speaker.

After that 30 minutes, you've learned a great deal about your friend's crisis and how to be a supportive friend. You've learned nothing from the speaker, because they did not have your attention. Learning requires attention.

One of the ways that we can use videos is as a hook to grab students' attention. This applies to either online or flipped classrooms. Either way, think of the video as a teaser, an attention-grabber, or a *hook*, as we say in the writing world.

Let's stick with the previous example and imagine that the speaker opens the session with a one-liner that is so powerful that it stops you in your tracks. You feel your phone vibrate, but the speaker so enthralls you that you decide that you'll ignore the text until after the speech. The speaker's hook grabbed your attention and won't let go. You're ready to learn. You give the speaker your complete attention and participate in a valuable learning experience. You text your friend when the conference is over.

Hooks are small and precise. They're quick. This type of video will be less than 30 seconds, and you'll use it to grab your students' attention. That might mean that you'll ask them a challenging question, share a cool fact about your subject matter, or direct them to consider a topic in light of their own past experiences. Whatever approach you take, your focus here is on getting your students' attention.

Using videos to grab attention will help activate students' prior knowledge on a topic and will keep their attention focused on the work to come. Have fun with these types of videos and be creative. Challenge yourself to create short videos that will pique students' interest. This focused approach will force you to more deeply consider the core elements of the lesson, making this an exercise that will benefit both you and your students.

TIP 17: MAKE A MINI-LECTURE

◀◀ I ▶▶

In the age of active learning, many land-based teachers are spending less time lecturing their students. Lecture still has its place in higher education though, and I've found that mini-lectures are the best of both worlds. By mini-lecture I mean limiting the time that I spend lecturing to 10-minute increments. This is based on my observations of people's attention spans and recommendations from John Medina (2008), an expert on neuroeducation and author of the book *Brain Rules*.

In my years of working with online faculty, I've noticed that lectures are often absent from online courses. A curious example of this that I've seen used by many online teachers is to post a set of PowerPoint slides and title them as the week's lecture. No audio. No video. Just text-heavy slides. Is that a lecture? Not in my book.

I've also seen instructors post so-called lecture notes, which are Word documents filled with written text on a topic. Again, that's not a substitute for a lecture. My hunch is that these teachers recognize the need to share their professional expertise with students, but no one has ever supported them in creating instructional, lecture-style videos.

By definition, a *lecture* is a talk or speech. Lectures, when done well, are a valuable pedagogical tool in both land-based and online courses. If you haven't included any lectures in your online courses, this is an excellent way to make use of videos. Which topics in your course would be most worthy of a lecture?

When creating videos of a mini-lecture, remember to keep your video to about 10 minutes. If your topic requires more time, identify subtopics and record more than a single video. Breaking up the content like this will make the videos easier to follow, and they'll better align with the attention span of the average person. Typically, you'll want to record these as headshot videos, screencasts, or a combination of both. You'll learn more about how to make that decision in Section Four.

Ideally, you'll introduce some interactive elements into your mini-lecture videos. For example, ask questions throughout your video. If you're using a PowerPoint along with your lecture, include these questions on your slides. Encourage students to jot down their answers or suggest that they pause the video and speak their responses out loud. You can also ask students to take notes during your lectures and to develop one question that they have about your lecture. They can then post their questions to a course discussion. This will help to ensure that students are paying attention and feel engaged in the lecture.

In short, lecture in higher education has a bit of the Goldilocks syndrome. We use too much of it in land-based teaching and not enough of it in online learning. Let's bring some balance back into the equation by adding real, well-designed lectures into our online classrooms.

Reference

Medina, J. (2008). *Brain rules: 12 principles for surviving and thriving at work, home, and school*. Seattle, WA: Pear Press.

TIP 18: TAKE STUDENTS ON A TOUR

◀◀ I ▶▶

I've made many different types of videos for various reasons in the years that I've been teaching online. One of the types of videos that I've found to be most effective and beneficial to student learning and engagement is a video tour of course modules. In a course with 10 modules, for example, I create 10 videos, 1 per module.

These videos are screencast videos, meaning I record my screen, which is set up to focus on the module of the week. Using my preferred video creation tool (tip 83), I am then able to also add a headshot-style video that captures my face and me talking about the content. This is the best of both worlds, because the students can see the course content and they're also able to see me, building a sense of connection between us.

In a module tour, I will welcome students to that module and introduce the topic. Typically, I'll begin with a quick story or anecdote on that topic to capture students' attention and to activate their prior knowledge, a common evidence-based teaching strategy. For example, if I'm teaching a module on note-taking, I'll tell students about how I took notes in college (poorly or not at all) and how my note-taking strategies have evolved. I might ask them to take a moment to think of one word that best describes their current note-taking approach.

I also make sure to highlight the relevance of the week's topic. Many of our online students are working adults, and relevance of course materials is essential to their motivation. I'll explain how the topic will help them in college, career, and their personal lives.

Then I'll begin to navigate through the module on my screen. I'll use the cursor to point out how they will access the module. For example, I'll say, "As always, we're going to access this week's module by clicking on Module 1 in the menu." I'll then review the learning objectives for the week and any required assignments.

Keeping videos to about 5 to 10 minutes in length forces me to stay on topic and to decide the priorities for these videos. That means that I might not go over every task in the module in detail, but I will focus on the key tasks that I think are most important for successful completion of the module. If I can't keep the content below 10 minutes, I will sometimes make a second video that focuses on a specific assignment as needed.

Since many of our online courses include discussions, and since those discussions are often the heart of our courses, I will make sure to review the discussion prompt and to offer success tips to students. My videos include lots of examples of how students can approach the required assignments. Many learners (myself included) need examples to best understand new concepts.

I end these videos with words of encouragement and a reminder to students to contact me with any questions. As always, I keep the videos general so that they are sustainable (see tip 63). I don't mention specific due dates (e.g., "Your initial post to the discussion is due on March 27th"). Instead, I might say, "Your initial post to the discussion is due on Thursday." That way, I can be sure that I'm able to reuse the video in a future term. If you always use the same day of the week for due dates, this will suffice. If you want to keep your due date options open, you can say, "Please see the syllabus for assignment due dates."

Course module tours are the epitome of the simple and sustainable model that you are learning about in this book. They're easy to make because you don't need to prepare any script—just walk students through that section of the course and record it. They're sustainable and can be reused each term; once you invest the time in creating them, they'll continue to serve you and your students for many terms to come.

If creating a video for each module of your course seems too daunting, start with developing one module tour for the first module. This is the part of the course where many students are very overwhelmed and could most benefit from additional support. Then you can add more modules in future terms.

TIP 19: USE GRAPHIC ORGANIZERS TO CONNECT IDEAS

◀◀ ▌ ▶▶

A couple of terms into my teaching career, I started to grimace every time I looked at my syllabus. I imagined it from a student's point of view— a dense collection of written text repeating a bunch of rules. *How dull*, I realized. *There's got to be a better way*. After doing a bit of research, I found information about how to use a graphic syllabus, a visual display of course content showing connections between and among ideas. While I still kept most of the written portion of the syllabus, I added a graphic organizer (i.e., a concept map or mind map) that showed students all of the major course concepts, their connections to one another, and the why or relevance of each of these concepts. I even splurged on color printing for this page of the syllabus.

Sharing this graphic organizer with my students felt great; it was a chance to be creative, but I also sensed that I was explaining the course to them much more effectively. Where else can I use this tool, I wondered?

Since then, I've continued to weave graphic organizers into my teaching, and as an aside, I use them constantly in my writing, mostly to brainstorm and outline essays.

It was only after years of using graphic organizers to show students connections among ideas that I began to understand the science behind them. John Medina (2008) explains how our brains prefer to receive meaning before details. Providing context via visuals supports the learning process.

Including graphic organizers in your videos is a great way to engage your students and harness what we know about how the brain learns best. Often, because we are very knowledgeable about our fields of study, it's easy for us to dive right into the details. Our students, however, need us to keep a beginner's mind and to explain meaning before details. One way to do this is to create a graphic organizer of the topic that you want to cover in your video and use it in a screencast to explain the concept.

I currently use a tool called Bubbl (n.d.) to develop graphic organizers. I hope that Bubbl stays with us for a very long time, but technology comes and goes. If not, a simple Internet search for "graphic organizers" or "concept mapping tools" will turn up several options for you. Of course, you could also draw a simple graphic organizer by hand, scan it with your phone or scanner, and use that image as the foundation of a video. Whatever tool you use, your students will benefit from the chance to see how details connect with the larger meaning of your content.

References

Bubbl. (n.d.) *Home*. Retrieved from https://bubbl.us/

Medina, J. (2008). *Brain rules: 12 principles for surviving and thriving at work, home, and school*. Seattle, WA: Pear Press.

TIP 20: WELCOME WEEK

◀◀ I ▶▶

Many students who attend a land-based institution and take traditional courses are welcomed to campus at the start of each new term by a series of events often referred to as "Welcome Week" or something similar. These events, activities, and workshops are a way to set students up for a successful term, communicate our care for them, and build peer-to-peer and student/faculty/staff connections. Why don't we offer the same type of welcome to our online students?

One of the ways that you might wish to use videos in your online course is through designing a welcome week. For land-based educators, you might also decide to create your very own welcome week for your course. Aim for a series of five to seven videos that you will release through your learning management system daily during that week, consistently branding the videos with the language of "Welcome Week" to communicate your values and goals to your students.

What sorts of topics will you include in your welcome videos? Consider the following possibilities:

- Faculty introduction
- A story about why you are teaching this course or this topic
- Syllabus review
- Course navigation
- Top 10 strategies to succeed in your course
- Suggestions for online support services (e.g., tutoring), including both internal and external resources

Using a welcome week format will front-load critical information and communicate to your students that the online learning experience is not second-best to land-based options. Many of the things that make the college experience engaging for land-based students can be done online as well. We also have things that we can do online that can't be done in a traditional setting. For example, while many students might not be able to access traditional welcome week activities in person due to time constraints, our online students will have asynchronous and flexible access to our welcome week videos.

How can you welcome students to your online institution and your course? What information would have helped your previous students succeed? By creating your own welcome week, your students will be well prepared and know that you care about their success—a recipe for a great start to a new course.

TIP 21: GREET STUDENTS AT THE DOOR

◄◄ ❚ ►►

One of my favorite pieces of education research in recent years involves, positive greetings at the door, or PGDs. This study found that when teachers met students at the door with a positive welcome at the start of class, students fared better during that class period and teachers spent less time on behavior management allowing more time for instruction (Terada, 2018). As soon as I read that article, I started to think about how to translate this concept into the online learning environment.

How can we greet students at the door of our online courses? While the asynchronous format of most online courses negates the possibility of a personal greeting before every "class," could we replicate the main idea of the study using videos? What would it look like to offer students this type of greeting?

One way to greet students would be to create a short video explaining this research and telling students that you want to greet them at the door, too. Let them know how you plan to welcome them to the start of a new module or week. That initial video could introduce the concept, and then you could switch to a written greeting in the form of weekly announcements or e-mails. Another option would be to follow the introductory video with weekly video greetings.

If you teach small land-based sections, you might choose to use this research for in-person greetings at the start of class. What if you teach larger classes, maybe even huge lectures, and greeting individual students is not possible? Could you create a short video welcome at the start of each week that you e-mail to students about 10 minutes before your class starts? We know students are probably poking around on their phones as they wait for class to begin. Why not use that time to welcome them with a video?

This is a great model for anyone who wants to prioritize relationship building. There are a variety of ways that you can approach this model from a logistical standpoint; the important thing is to keep the heart of the model at the center of your approach. The goal is to let students know that you care and connect with them individually on a consistent (ideally weekly) basis.

Where is the "door" of your online classroom? How can you meet students there and welcome them into your course?

Reference

Terada, Y. (2018). Welcoming students with a smile. Edutopia. Retrieved from https://www.edutopia.org/article/welcoming-students-smile

TIP 22: PLAY A GAME

◀◀ ▐ ▶▶

Game-based learning has taken off in recent years, but games in the classroom aren't new (Isaacs, 2015). I can recall playing games at school from the very start of my educational journey. Perhaps what is new is the term itself, *game-based learning*, and our increasing knowledge of how games can support how our brains learn best by creating fun, novel, and challenging learning experiences.

I'll share a quick story to illustrate my take on using games in the college classroom. Once, when I was teaching a land-based course, I brought clickers into the classroom for a midterm review exercise. For those not familiar with clickers, each student had a handheld device that allowed them to select answers to trivia-type questions. In the game that I chose for them, those who had the most correct answers would see their car race to the head of the pack on a racetrack, projected on a screen at the front of the classroom. I introduced the game by reminding students that it was just for fun and to not worry too much about winning or losing.

At the end of class, one of my students approached me. She was an introverted student who rarely spoke in class unless it was in one-on-one or small-group activities.

"I loved that," she said softly.

I thought I'd misheard her. "I'm sorry?"

"I said I loved that. It was so much fun." A huge grin broke across her face, something I hadn't seen before.

"Wow, I'm so glad," I said, patting myself on the back.

She filed out of the room, and another student came up to the podium as I packed up the clickers.

"I hated that," he said. "It was too stressful."

"Okey-dokey," I said. "Good to know."

Well, I guess the win there was that my students felt comfortable expressing their opinions to me. It also illustrates my take on game-based learning. As with many of the teaching strategies that we use, it's motivating for some students and frustrating for others. I see games in the classroom like salt— use with moderation.

If you want to explore game-based teaching, consider how you can use videos to create a very simple gaming experience. One example of this is to create an online scavenger hunt. I've used this lesson in my first-year experience courses, but it's a great introductory exercise in any course. Give students a list of items to find in your online classroom (or for land-based teachers, in any supplementary online learning environment). Students can take screenshots of the items or copy and paste the URL into a document for submission.

Another simple example is to phrase an assignment using the language of a game or quest. Explain to students that they are trying to solve a puzzle or be the hero or heroine of the game. If, for example, you are going to require a quiz on the digestive system in your online biology course, what if instead of calling it a quiz, you call it a trivia challenge? You could let students know that the winner of the challenge will be able to select the discussion topic for the next week from a list of predetermined topics.

Some teachers like to gamify their feedback to students. Let students know that you will be hiding a secret code within your written feedback to them. Tell them that if they send you the secret code by a certain date, you'll reward them with a prize. Prizes can be a few extra credit points on an assignment or more choices on an upcoming assignment.

Use videos to introduce games, explain their relevance, and list any rules. For the game lovers among you, this is a fun and simple exercise to get students active and engaged. While the scavenger hunt model is the most simple and sustainable approach, be creative here. You might think of other games that fit better with your teaching style or course content.

Whichever approach you choose, my advice is to start small and to be mindful that the games remain low stakes. We want to find that sweet spot where the competition is exciting without becoming stressful. Finally, be intentional about your use of games. In general, games should support your instructional goals. That said, developing classroom community is a worthy goal, so including games that help students bond and connect, just for fun, can be a good use of gamification as well.

Reference

Isaacs, S. (2015). *The difference between gamification and game-based learning*. ASCD Inservice. Retrieved from http://inservice.ascd.org/the-difference-between-gamification-and-game-based-learning/

TIP 23: IT'S TIME FOR A FIELD TRIP

◀◀ I ▶▶

The videos that you create don't have to be limited to your home office. Another option is to take your students on a video field trip. This is a great way to introduce novelty into your classroom, which is important because we know that our brains don't pay attention to boring things; adding novelty helps us gain and keep students' interest in support of learning (Hardiman, 2012).

One concept that I'll often teach my students is biophilia, which relates to focus, a critical college success skill. Biophilia is the idea that views of nature (or even better, being in nature) improve our focus and make us feel better (Torres, 2015). Pay attention the next time you're in an airport or hospital: You'll probably notice large pictures of nature in those spaces.

To bring this concept to my students, I once created a video to remind them to take a break and look outside or to go for a walk as part of their study routine. I could've recorded that video in my home office and perhaps done a screencast including some nice pictures of trees. Instead, I carried my tripod and phone into my backyard, where I sat on a big boulder and encouraged students to go outside to improve their concentration. This quick field trip showed students what I most wanted them to learn, rather than just telling them. It also felt good for me to express my creativity in that way.

Teach nutrition? Record a video of yourself looking at food labels in the grocery store. Poetry? Quietly (shhh!) record a video in the poetry section of your local library. Art? Visit your local art museum and grab a quick video to show students the cultural offerings that might be available in their local communities. If you have the time and energy to plan special trips to record your videos, go for it. If not, I bet you regularly visit places that might be well suited for this type of video and may realize it in the middle of a trip. Just remember to bring your smartphone with you.

Field trips are a great way to provide information, to connect, and to express your creativity through your instructional videos. Where could you take your students?

References

Hardiman, M. (2012). *The brain-targeted teaching model for 21st century schools.* Thousand Oaks, CA: SAGE.

Torres, N. (2015). Gazing at nature makes you more productive: An interview with Kate Lee. *Harvard Business Review.* Retrieved from https://hbr.org/2015/09/gazing-at-nature-makes-you-more-productive

SECTION THREE

GUIDING THEORIES AND RESEARCH

Many of you reading this book took an educational theory course at some point during graduate school. Others had a graduate school experience focused on your discipline, not on teaching, and may not have been specifically exposed to educational theories. Either way, I believe that it's important to have some theories to guide our work. In the words generally attributed to Kurt Lewin, "There is nothing so practical as a good theory."

I love theories. I'm a big-picture person, so theories help me get a foundation of understanding that leads me to make practical decisions in my daily work. Luckily, there's no shortage of theories in the world of higher education.

This section was such a gift for me to write because I was able to dive into some of my most-loved theories and models, all of which have been profoundly influential in my work in higher education. I hope that this will give you a strong foundation for your video development process. Beyond your work with video, though, I can imagine that this section might influence your teaching on a broader level. I've pulled a wide range of theories for you to consider, so as you read, don't limit your outlook to videos alone. Think big and let the power of theory lead you into new teaching terrain.

As a result of the tips in this section, you will build a theoretical framework for your approach to videos. This is also a great section for any of you who feel like you might need to defend your use of videos or your decision to take a simple and sustainable approach. These tips will give you a language to call on in your conversations about videos. Finally, my greatest hope for this work would be that some of you will begin writing and sharing your ideas about teaching with videos. If so, these tips will give you a solid background to develop your own models and to share them with the world.

TIP 24: BE PRESENT WITH THE COMMUNITY OF INQUIRY MODEL

◄◄ I ►►

Online education is still in its infancy. While our body of theoretical frameworks is growing, one model stands out as the foremost in our field: the community of inquiry (CoI) model. Garrison, Anderson, and Archer developed the model in 2000, and there is now a robust online warehouse of CoI research and information housed on the Athabasca University website that's worth checking out (Athabasca University, n.d.). CoI is one of the models that has been most influential in my teaching as an online educator.

The CoI model is built around the concept of presence, with three types of presence identified as being critical to the online learning experience: cognitive presence, social presence, and teaching presence. Cognitive presence relates to our ability to craft opportunities for learners to engage with course content and to seek and discover meaning in their learning journeys. Social presence pertains to interpersonal relationships and a sense of being part of a community. Teaching presence is a bit more nebulous, but I equate it to being the captain of a ship or the head of a household. It is the ability of a teacher to reveal themselves as a capable leader in the online classroom, managing, facilitating, and participating in the learning experience.

Many online educators consider their teaching choices in light of the intersections between social and teaching presence. How present are you in your online classroom? What strategies do you use to exhibit your presence to and with your students? One way to better understand presence is by considering its opposite: absence.

I have been a student in many online courses, and I've had a variety of professors. If I were to categorize them, I'd say that 50% have been top-notch faculty with powerful presence. Another 49% were just okay—average online teachers with minimal presence. That leaves only 1%. After having taken many online courses, there is just one professor who stands out as awful. What made him so? He just wasn't there. He didn't post announcements, didn't participate in the discussion, and returned assignments three weeks after the due date with very few, if any, comments. In short, a robot could've done a better job of teaching that course. In online learning, absence does not make students' hearts grow fonder.

Most of my teachers have been very present in my online courses, and presence is a guiding force in my own teaching. In addition to strategies like posting regular course announcements, using e-mail, facilitating the discussion, and sharing engaging and compelling course content, videos are one of the primary ways that I build a strong presence as an online teacher.

I have taught with and without videos; while my students don't use the language of the CoI model in their communications with me or in their student evaluations, in the video-infused courses that I teach, students will often say things such as, "I thought that I wouldn't get to know my professor at all, but I feel like I really know Karen," or "I love how Karen took the time to create weekly videos for us. I feel like she really cares about our success." Videos have helped me become more present for my students. Because I take the time to make videos, creating a strong online teaching presence, even though our classroom doesn't have four walls, my students know that I am in it with them.

How do you demonstrate presence in your online courses? How can you use this model to support your video creation practice?

Reference

Athabasca University. (n.d.) The community of inquiry. Retrieved from coi .athabascau.ca

TIP 25: VALIDATE YOUR STUDENTS

◀◀ I ▶▶

Most of those who have studied higher education theories are familiar with the work of Vincent Tinto (1993), whose theory of academic and social integration and their relationship to student attrition is one of the foremost in the field. Tinto argues that when students are integrated, both academically and socially, into the culture of a campus, they are more likely to persist.

While Tinto is a major scholar in our field, I have found that his ideas don't always seem to fit my students, most of whom are older adult learners with children and jobs, many of them also first-generation students from diverse backgrounds. Higher education professionals have long referred to these students as nontraditional, because for many years, they were. Today, these students are no longer the exception to the rule. To guide my work with new-traditional students, I rely heavily on the work of Laura Rendon (1994) and her validation theory.

Rendon spoke to new-traditional students and sought to understand what factors helped these students persist and succeed in college. Students talked about the power of a caring adult on campus in helping them stay on course. In short, when someone on campus, a faculty member, adviser, or other staff person, validated the student, assuring them that they belonged on campus and that they were, in fact, a college student, the student was motivated to succeed.

Here's my short version of validation theory in action: "You can do this, and I am going to help you."

Rendon's theory guides my use of videos. One of the primary ways that I use videos is to validate and motivate my students. Sometimes I'll create a video to tell my students that I see their hard work and to remind them that they aren't alone. Validation can be the sole purpose of a video. Other times, I will include validating messages alongside other content. For example, I might create a video to explain that week's discussion prompt in more detail, but I'll also make sure to include words of encouragement in the video, reminding students that they can do it, and that I'm available to help them.

If the only action that you take is to create a brief welcome video for the first week of your course, telling students that you believe in them and that you're going to help them on their journey, I would argue that you've made a transformational leap in your teaching. For our new-traditional students, validation is critical and can mean the difference between dropping out and persisting. Validation is not only great for our students but also simple and sustainable for us. Weaving a few kind words throughout your videos is so easy to do and takes very little time. It will help your students and empower you as a teacher when you see the power of validation in action.

References

Rendon, L. (1994). Validating culturally diverse students: Toward a new model of learning and student development. *Innovative Higher Education, 19*(1), 33–51.

Retrieved   from   https://www.csuchico.edu/ourdemocracy/_assets/documents/
pedagogy/rendon,-l.-1994---validation-theory.pdf

Tinto, V. (1993). *Leaving college: Rethinking the causes and cures of student attrition.*
Chicago, IL: University of Chicago Press.

TIP 26: BEGIN WITH BRAINS

◀◀ I ▶▶

When I started teaching, I tore through as much research as I could find to help me become a better teacher. I was quickly drawn to the work of Eric Jensen (2005) on brain-based teaching and learning. The idea behind brain-based teaching and learning is to use our growing knowledge of how the brain works, learns, and thrives, born out of astounding advances in the field of neuroscience in the past 30 years, to inform our teaching. There are now multiple ways to describe this approach, including brain-targeted teaching; neuroeducation; and mind, brain, and education science. Proponents of each will argue that there are important distinctions in these naming conventions. Academia loves to name things, but for the purposes of this book, we'll keep it simple and use the term *brain-based teaching* or *BBT*.

This tip will help you understand how the use of videos aligns with what we know about how the brain learns best. Let's focus on two critical aspects of BBT: gaining attention through novelty and creating multisensory learning environments. By understanding each of these concepts, you'll have an excellent foundation to guide your use of videos.

First, let's talk about attention. Our brains evolved to notice novel events in our environment (think of a flash of orange in a forest of green and why it's crucial to our survival to see that). Boring and repetitive learning environments fail to capture our attention. In a text-heavy online course, a video stands out as novel; it will catch your students' attention, allowing you to impart important ideas and information. Mariale Hardiman (2012), an expert on the brain and learning, writes, "Regular changes in the learning environment seem to be an effective tool for capturing attention and providing visual stimulation" (p. 62). Videos are a way we can capture attention in an online classroom.

Second, let's discuss multisensory learning. John Medina (2008) keeps it simple with this rule: "Vision trumps all other senses" (p. 221). This relates to a well-known design principle called the pictorial superiority effect which is a fancy way of saying that a picture is worth a thousand words. "When it comes to memory," Medina says, "researchers have known for more than 100 years that pictures and text follow very different rules. The more visual the input becomes, the more likely it is to be recognized—and recalled" (p. 233). Videos create a strong visual that will capture your students' attention more effectively than text.

It is gratifying to know that when we invest our time in creating videos for our students, we are not only applying an effective teaching strategy but also using pedagogical choices that the latest neuroscience research supports. Our brains learn best when engaged with novelty and when presented with images. Your videos will represent BBT in action.

Position your smartphone's camera over Figure 26.1 to view a video about this tip.

Figure 26.1. Video: *Begin With Brains.*

Note. Retrieved from https://youtu.be/J-1Skpe1NSE

References

Hardiman, M. (2012). *The brain-targeted teaching model for 21st century schools.* Thousand Oaks, CA: SAGE.

Jensen, E. (2005). *Teaching with the brain in mind.* Alexandria, VA: ASCD.

Medina, J. (2008). *Brain rules: 12 principles for surviving and thriving at work, home, and school.* Seattle, WA: Pear Press.

TIP 27: GO THE DISTANCE

◀◀ ❙ ▶▶

I've been teaching online since 2007, and in the past year, I've started to feel like one of the old-timers of online learning. If you're like me, you might recall that when you first started teaching online, some people were still regularly using the phrases *distance education* or *distance learning*. This covered not only courses that took place online but also correspondence courses where students and their teachers mailed hard copy work and assignments back and forth to one another. Yes, when I started teaching, a couple of correspondence courses were still being offered at my institution. As I said, I'm one of the old-timers.

One of the first theories to develop around distance education was Moore's theory of transactional distance. It is based on the idea that when learners and teachers are not in the same time or space, profound differences occur in the teaching and learning experience. "With separation there is a psychological and communications space to be crossed, a space of potential misunderstanding between the inputs of instructor and those of the learner. It is this psychological and communications space that is the transactional distance" (Moore, 1997, para. 2).

I often hear people claim that "good teaching is good teaching, no matter the modality." I agree. *And* teaching online is different from land-based teaching because of the need to cross this transactional distance. This is the paradox of online teaching: It is at once the same as and different from its traditional counterpart. It takes more intentional effort to communicate and connect with our students online.

Videos are one of my primary methods for bridging this distance with my students. Imagine a student in an online course with no video component. There might be one picture of the instructor in the instructor's profile (which the student might never see). The student's only communication with the teacher takes place via written text. Do you sense the transactional distance inherent in that relationship?

Now, consider a course infused with even one video, perhaps a welcome video to start the class off with a welcoming tone. Picture those students, curled up on their couches, in their cars at school pickup waiting for their kids, or on a lunch break from work, watching a video of their professor introducing herself and describing the goals of the course. The transactional distance has been lessened. For those three minutes, video brings those students closer to their professor.

This is one of the foundational theories of online education, and it speaks forcefully to the value of video in the online classroom. Do you sense the distance between yourself and your students when you teach online? How can you use videos to come closer to your students?

Reference

Moore, M. (1997). Theory of transactional distance. In D. Keegan (Ed.), *Theoretical principles of distance education* (pp. 22–38). New York, NY: Routledge. Retrieved from http://www.c3l.uni-oldenburg.de/cde/found/moore93.pdf

TIP 28: IN THIS TOGETHER

◄◄ I ►►

I love informing my work in higher education with noneducational theories. One of those theories comes from the field of biology. Warning: You may experience a flashback to your ninth-grade biology class as you read through this tip.

The concept of symbiotic relationships describes three types of relationships between organisms: parasitism, commensalism, and mutualism. In parasitism, one organism is helped while the other is harmed (e.g., tick feeding off your dog). In commensalism, one organism is helped, and the other is neither helped nor harmed. This is a more neutral relationship. Finally, we arrive at my favorite: mutualism, a relationship in which both organisms benefit.

This model has helped me to better understand the social relationships between students, faculty, and institutions. Are my students worse off, better off, or not impacted at all due to my teaching? My goal as a teacher is always to leave my students better off than they were when they found me. My biggest fear as a teacher is that I will further disadvantage students who are already disadvantaged. I actively work against this in my teaching and in the faculty development and advocacy work that I do in higher education. As an industry, I would argue that we should aim for a model of mutuality, where students, faculty, staff, and institutions are all helping one another be better.

This model of creating simple and sustainable videos relies on the concept of mutualism. Many models of teaching, I've noticed, don't look at how the teaching experience can benefit teachers. We often argue that faculty should sacrifice themselves on behalf of their students, becoming martyrs to their students' success. I don't think that any human can sustain this type of constant self-sacrifice. In my experience and observations, it leads to burnout. Further, my big-picture goal is to help make the world a better place. Even if we believe that faculty self-sacrifice could lead to better student outcomes, then we would be left with the problem of thousands of ruined teachers and faculty.

Mutualism offers another way forward. Videos, I believe, benefit both teachers and students, benefits that I'll continue to describe throughout this book. As you move forward in your video creation journey, pay attention to the benefits and costs of using video for both you and your students. As needed, course-correct your approach to return to a symbiotic relationship based on mutual benefits.

TIP 29: APPLY AESTHETIC-USABILITY EFFECT

◄◄ I ►►

One of the fields of study that has influenced my online teaching and video content creation is design. Design theory helps engage my creative intuition as a teacher; plus, it's just cool and fun. I love that a lot of design theory isn't focused specifically on education; I think it's important that we seek ideas from other fields.

Aesthetic-usability effect is a basic design principle that can help us understand why videos might be so effective in the online classroom. It maintains that our perception of how something looks (i.e., whether we find it pleasing to the eye) influences our perception of how easy (or difficult) it will be to use that item (Lidwell, Holden, & Butler, 2003). If we perceive something to be aesthetically pleasing, we believe that it will be easy to use. If we perceive something as aesthetically displeasing, we think that it will be difficult to use.

The first time I discovered this theory, I immediately thought of how I use images and videos in my online courses, whether in fully online courses or online course shells that complement a land-based course. As a student or end-user, I find images and video thumbnails more attractive to my eye than a page loaded with text. Was that also true for my students?

I teach primarily first-term college students, many of whom aren't just new to college, they're also new to online learning—a double whammy. Part of my job is to help them transition into the world of online higher education. I believe that videos help ease that transition for many reasons, including their visual appeal. If creating a visually pleasing class leads new students to believe that a class is less difficult, that seems like a definite benefit of videos to me.

Now that you've learned the basics of aesthetic-usability effect, start to notice your reactions to content in your online travels. Are you drawn to videos and images? Do videos and images give you the sense that the content will be easier to use? By starting to observe your reactions to the relationship between aesthetics and usability, you'll be better prepared to articulate the value of videos in your teaching and to use this design principle throughout your teaching, such as in designing an aesthetically pleasing syllabus.

Reference

Lidwell, W., Holden, K., & Butler, J. (2003). *Universal principles of design: 125 ways to enhance usability, influence perception, increase appeal, make better design decisions, and teach through design.* Beverly, MA: Rockport Publishers.

TIP 30: FIGHT FEAR

◀◀ I ▶▶

Do you ever feel as if students are their own worst enemies? As if they make confounding decisions that work against their own best interests? You aren't alone. Rebecca Cox (2009), author of *The College Fear Factor*, set out to better understand college students, specifically investigating the experiences of first-generation college students and their professors.

Cox studied a group of community college students enrolled in various sections of a first-year composition course. She spoke extensively to the students as well as their professors. Cox found that the students she studied utilized a series of self-protective behaviors to defend their sense of self in the college classroom. Rather than being proven as unworthy of being in college, for example, students might instead choose to not turn in an assignment. To a student whose sense of self as a college student rests on shaky ground, avoidance feels preferable to being "discovered" as an imposter.

Cox's book floored me when I first read it. The stories she shares resonated with many of my own experiences as a teacher. I was able to see that it wasn't a lack of motivation that often stood in the way of my students' success but, rather, fear. This was a significant shift for me as an educator, and it's a theory that I still carry with me and use regularly.

Videos are a great way to help students overcome the fear factor. Critically, you can use videos to explain assignments and expectations (see tip 14) clearly. Many first-generation college students might not be aware of a lot of our higher ed lingo. By explaining things in a video in addition to written directions and a rubric, students have a better chance of fully understanding an assignment. Also, you can use videos to help students notice their fears and take action rather than passively avoiding challenging situations. One of my teaching philosophies is to name the elephant in the room. Talk to students about these issues and their fears. Students can and should be active participants in their education.

In addition to explaining assignments, consider using videos to dispel fears. Tell students a story (see tip 15) about a time when you failed at something and how the experience helped you grow. If you don't have a great failure story, not to worry. Most famous folks have a wealth of failure stories that you can discover with a simple Internet search. Share those stories with students, reminding them that we can choose to learn from our challenges. They aren't failures; they are opportunities.

Use videos to let students know that you are available to help them. I am very direct about encouraging students to seek me out for help. Instead of saying, "Let me know if you have any questions," I will often say, "What questions do you have? Please contact me with those questions. I love getting questions from students because I love to help people. Your question will make me happy, because it will give me a chance to help."

You could also use your videos to list frequently asked questions that you've received from past students. Create a classroom culture where students know that it's better to ask than to avoid. Stand with your students through your videos, facing fear head-on.

Reference

Cox, R. (2009). *The college fear factor.* Cambridge, MA: Harvard University Press.

TIP 31: GET EMOTIONAL

◄◄ ❙ ►►

Many of us were taught to leave our emotions at the door when we entered a college classroom, whether as a teacher or a student. "We're here to teach (or learn), not to talk about feelings."

Take a minute to sit with this idea. What does that even look like? Do we detach a part of ourselves, our hearts or limbic systems, and set them in a designated cubby at the start of class, only to pick them back up on the way out?

The idea that human beings can coat-check their emotions doesn't hold up to logic. Indeed, it's contradicted by everything that science knows about the human brain. Emotions are not only a critical part of who we are but also fundamental to our higher order thinking processes. In short, if we are disconnected from our emotions, we don't think as well (Damasio, 1994). The most rational thinking is born of a healthy connection to one's emotions. Rather than trying to create emotion-free zones in our classrooms, an impossible task anyway, the brain and learning sciences tell us that we should be intentionally harnessing the power of emotions to create richer learning experiences (Cavanagh, 2016).

Videos help me integrate emotions into my teaching. I talk to my students about the emotional process of transitioning into life as a first-year college student. For example, each term that I teach, I always encounter several students who tell me in the first week of our course that they are feeling anxious about starting college. I always respond by saying the same thing, "It's okay to be a bit anxious. It's totally normal. In fact, it's not a bad thing. It shows that you care about your success." I try to normalize their frustration, showing them that it's not a sign that they don't belong in college, but rather a common part of being a college student. Since I'm almost always taking a course here or there myself, I tell them how I get nervous and frustrated too when starting something new.

Bring emotions into your videos. Notice and share yours (in an appropriate manner). Talk about how your emotions have challenged you and how you navigated that challenge. By creating a positive and supportive classroom climate that accepts and celebrates the inevitability of emotions, you're not only demonstrating care for your students but also priming their rational brains for their very best higher order thinking.

References

Cavanagh, S. R. (2016). *The spark of learning: Energizing the college classroom with the science of emotion.* Morgantown: West Virginia University Press.

Damasio, A. (1994). *Descartes' error: Emotion, reason, and the human brain.* New York, NY: Putnam.

TIP 32: CULTIVATE COMMONALITIES

◀◀ ❙ ▶▶

I'm a big fan of podcasts. I love listening to them at the gym, which is a great combination of body and mind exercise. Recently, I listened to a podcast that pointed me toward some research that beautifully illustrates how I use videos in my online classroom. *Hidden Brain* podcast host Shankar Vedantum interviewed educational researcher Hunter Gehlbach about his study on student–teacher connections (Penman, 2015). Gehlbach and his team performed a study in which they collected information about students' and teachers' interests. Then, researchers facilitated the sharing of common points of interest between the teachers and students. This group was compared to a control group. The discovery of common interests was correlated with positive outcomes for both students and teachers, with particularly strong positive impacts noted for "at-risk" or marginalized populations.

Gehlbach's study points to the potential of being more intentional about cultivating positive student–faculty relationships. Although this study was performed in a K–12 setting, it offers exciting possibilities for our work to improve the online learning experience for both students and teachers. Videos are well suited to support the discovery of common interests in the online learning environment.

One of the strategies that I've been using for years is to weave small details about myself into my videos. I might mention my dog, or my son, or a television show that I've been enjoying. Students can also make observations about my interests based on the setting of my video (there are usually many books in the background) or my appearance (Karen owns a lot of eyeglasses). For many years, this has been a purely intuitive practice.

Since discovering Gehlbach's research, I now realize that I've been cultivating commonalities by sharing small details about myself with my students. Keep in mind that these never need to be very personal details, and the level of detail that you're comfortable sharing will vary. Can you share your favorite food, color, or movie with your students? Could you tell them a story about a challenging educational experience or perceived failure? Think about some simple details that you can weave into your videos, knowing that this could potentially have a significant impact on the success of your students, particularly those most in need.

Reference

Penman, M. (2015, October 13). *In the classroom, common ground can transform GPAs* [Audio podcast]. Retrieved from https://www.npr.org/2015/10/13/444446708/ in-the-classroom-common-ground-can-transform-gpas

TIP 33: INTEGRATE IMMEDIACY CUES

◀◀ ▌ ▶▶

It's always a pleasantly curious feeling to happen upon a theory that explains a teaching practice that you've been using for years. I suppose that if an educational theory is sound, it makes sense that many teachers will already have been implementing it. It does feel a bit like looking in a funny mirror at an amusement park, though. "Is that me? Is that what I do? Is that what I look like?"

I had this feeling recently when I heard Sarah Rose Cavanagh (2019) speak at a conference on the topic of immediacy cues as part of her talk on using emotions in the college classroom. As Cavanagh described the various types of immediacy cues and gave the audience some background on the research supporting their use, I frantically scribbled in my notepad, "Immediacy cues in online learning!!!"

Cavanagh (2016) explains that "immediacy pertains to behaviors that are both spoken and unspoken and convey to students that you are interested in them, the material, and the process of learning" (p. 100). Without knowing it, it seems that I've made immediacy cues the heart of my teaching style for years. Some examples of immediacy cues listed by Cavanagh (2016) include "eye contact, leaning forward, smiling, a relaxed posture, use of gestures, a variety of vocal tones, and movement around the classroom" (p. 100). You'll find several of these woven into Section Seven, which focuses on presentation tips for your videos.

We can also, according to Cavanagh (2016), exhibit immediacy cues in our verbal choices, such as using the pronoun *we* to describe the work of the class, rather than *you* or *I*. One example of this is that I always address my students with the salutation, "Hello, Team." I'll describe the upcoming course content by saying, "This week, we are going to learn about . . ." I refer to "our course" rather than "my course." I use these verbal cues in my written text and my videos to consistently convey a sense of community and inclusivity. I want my students to know that we are in this work of higher education together and that they are never alone in their educational journey. I aim to cultivate a sense of shared responsibility for the teaching and learning process.

The concept of immediacy cues can support you in your video creation process. How do you communicate to students that you are a partner in the class experience? How can you demonstrate this through both verbal and nonverbal cues? Let this theory bring your awareness to your movements, facial expressions, and word choices when filming videos, and aim to bolster your use of immediacy cues in your teaching.

References

Cavanagh, S. R. (2016). *The spark of learning: Energizing the college classroom with the science of emotion.* Morgantown: West Virginia University Press.

Cavanagh, S. R. (2019, May 16). Investigating emotion-based interventions in the college classroom: Mindfulness and cognitive reappraisal. *Invitation to Learning: Emotions, Inclusivity, and Community.* Conference conducted at Assumption College, Worcester, Massachusetts.

TIP 34: KNOW THE RESEARCH

◀◀ I ▶▶

The body of research on the use of video in classrooms is limited but growing. This shouldn't surprise any of us, though, because both online learning and flipped classrooms are still in their infancy. That said, some promising research studies point to the potential benefits of video for student learning.

My philosophy on research is to be data informed, not data driven. I stay abreast of the current research in my field, I listen to my colleagues, and I value my own experiences. Taking all of that into account, I am entirely confident in the power of video to fuel both student and faculty success. Of course, information is power, so let's take a quick peek at some of the current research on videos to help you form your foundation for the work to come.

Screencasts (i.e., creating a video recording of your screen) have been found to improve performance in a remedial math course (Loch, Jordan, Lowe, & Mestel, 2014). In another study, instructional videos showed a moderate correlation to students' knowledge acquisition but an "overwhelmingly positive" correlation with students' perceptions of course quality (Morris & Chikwa, 2013, p. 25). Student satisfaction and course engagement levels increase with the use of instructor-generated videos (Draus, Curran, & Trempus, 2014) and graduate students reported that videos improved their connection with their instructor (Martin, Wang, & Sadaf, 2018). In a recent review, Michelle Pacansky-Brock (n.d.), a well-respected online educator known for her work on humanizing online learning, points to both videos and voice threads as an effective strategy to humanize our online courses. Finally, video was a commonly utilized teaching strategy in a recent survey of award-winning online faculty (Martin, Budhrani, Kumar, & Ritzhaupt, 2019).

While more research on the efficacy of educational videos is undoubtedly warranted, initial research supports using videos as a tool for student learning and success. Areas of investigation for future research could explore the ideal length and format for videos to meet a variety of instructional needs, the impact of videos on faculty success and satisfaction, and provide more detail on how videos impact the student-instructor relationship.

References

California State University. (n.d.). *Behaviors and strategies for improving online instructor presence.* Retrieved from http://page.teachingwithoutwalls.com/instructorpresencestrategiesci

Draus, P. J., Curran, M. J., & Trempus, M. S. (2014). The influence of instructor-generated video content on student satisfaction with and engagement in asynchronous online classes MERLOT. *Journal of Online Teaching and Learning, 10*(2), 240–254.

Loch, B., Jordan, C., Lowe, T., & Mestel, B. (2014). Do screencasts help to revise prerequisite mathematics? An investigation of student performance and perception. *International Journal of Mathematics Education, 45*(2), 256–268.

Martin, F., Budhrani, K., Kumar, S., & Ritzhaupt, A. (2019). Award-winning faculty online teaching practices: Roles and competencies. *Online Learning Journal, 23*(1), 184–205.

Martin, F., Wang, C., & Sadaf, A. (2018). Student perception of helpfulness of facilitation strategies that enhance instructor presence, connectedness, engagement, and learning in online courses. *The Internet and Higher Education, 37*, 52–65.

Morris, C., & Chikwa, G. (2013). Screencasts: How effective are they and how do students engage with them? *Active Learning in Higher Education, 15*(1), 25–37.

Pacansky-Brock, M. (n.d.) *How to humanize your online class.* Retrieved from https://www.brocansky.com/humanizing-infographic

SECTION FOUR

WHICH TYPES OF VIDEOS WILL WORK BEST FOR YOU?

un fact about me: In my work outside of higher education, I'm also a certified yoga teacher, and I've been practicing yoga since I was eight years old. My yoga teacher training program was based on hatha style and firmly grounded in the philosophy of yogic science. I remember one of my teachers saying that if she looked out into her yoga classes and everyone was doing something slightly different, she knew she'd done a good job as a teacher. She taught us that our job was not to create a class of cookie-cutter students and poses, but rather to inspire our students to become their own best teachers.

That teaching mind-set has crossed over from my work in yoga to my role as a higher educator. It also greatly informs this book. While we share similar challenges, every campus has a different culture. Within those cultures, various departments develop subcultures. Now, mix in a unique blend of students each term with your personality and teaching strengths. For me to argue for a one-size-fits-all model of using videos would deny all of those elements.

My job is to give you the best information that I can about teaching with videos and to make suggestions based on the research and my experience. Your job is to *discern* (that's an important word in the yoga world) which options are the best fit for you and your students. Just as a student in a yoga class might choose the more restful and passive child's pose over the active and engaging downward dog, you also have choices to make about the types of videos that will work best for you.

This section will help you consider the pros and cons of different types of videos. Most importantly, as a result of reading this section, you will be able to weigh the potential of each kind of video against your own needs and strengths. As you read through this section, remember to honor and prioritize your unique teaching needs at this time. By taking in this information and considering what will be the best fit for you, you'll be able to set yourself up for a successful video creation journey.

TIP 35: KEEP IT SIMPLE

◄◄ ❙ ►►

We live in interesting times. The Internet has opened up access to a level of information that is equally incredibly empowering and incredibly overwhelming to individuals. Knowledge is power, but ignorance is bliss. Further, most educators that I know are very busy individuals. This work is not only of the mind but also of the heart. We give a lot of ourselves in this field, and it's easy to watch our days quickly fill with a combination of teaching, service, and student support.

There are many different ways that you can approach making videos for your courses, and as many technological tools to support you in the process. If you chose to explore them all, weighing their pros and cons, you could easily lose days, weeks, months of your life in the pursuit of that level of knowledge. I know this because I've gone down that rabbit hole; the good news is that since I've already gone there and lived to tell about it, I can save you the time and trouble. The answer is to keep it simple.

Ironically, I've found that simplicity is often more difficult to practice than its polar opposite, complexity. When you start down the road of creating videos, shiny new edtech products will cross your path. You'll be tempted to provide your e-mail in exchange for e-books that will show you how to produce the best-looking videos in the biz. Someone on your campus or at a conference will try to shame you for not using the most advanced software available.

Ignore them all. If you follow this system, the one that I've been using for the past decade, you'll be creating high-quality, humanizing videos for years to come. You'll also enjoy doing it.

The temptation for more and more complexity will arise, often from external sources. Smile, nod, and whisper to yourself, "Simple and sustainable." Remember, we're playing the long game here: chess, not checkers. We are educators who are focused on building positive and supportive relationships with our students through the use of video. We care about not only the success of our students (something we're incredibly passionate about) but also our own success. We claim our right to be happy and supported in our work. We affirm our right to have a life outside of that work. We want to make videos, but we don't want the creation and maintenance of those videos to consume our lives.

Keeping it simple will be our mantra and guide. Write it down and post it in your workspace if need be. Let the rest of the world complexify. We will simplify.

TIP 36: FORGET HOLLYWOOD

◀◀ I ▶▶

Several years ago, I attended a conference geared toward online educators. I was there to learn, but I also presented a workshop for online teachers about how to create awesome instructional videos. The system that I shared with them in that presentation was the foundation for the work that I'm sharing with you in this book.

The day before I presented, I decided to check out another session on creating videos, hoping to pick up some new ideas and a fresh perspective. It was run by two men from a big university, both in size and prestige. I squeezed into a seat in the back row because the room was full.

"Students want Hollywood-level videos," the first presenter said. "Anything else is unacceptable and amateurish."

My eyes darted around the room. What had he just said? I sensed others stirring in their seats.

The presenters spent the next 45 minutes explaining their video production system, which required faculty to visit the campus studio (they had a fully loaded video production studio that probably rivaled many newsrooms) to create their videos, which were then edited by a production team.

There were very few questions, a lot of blank stares, and my gut tells me that the people who had come to that session with the hopes of gaining the requisite motivation to start creating videos left with less motivation than they'd started with. I took a deep breath and did a minute of soul searching before recommitting to my vision for my upcoming session.

The next day, my session was standing room only and filled with interaction and questions. I encouraged faculty to "break eggs to make omelets," to avoid using a script, to not worry too much about the technology, and to focus on having fun with videos. I heard from several folks in the following weeks about how they had taken the leap and started creating videos for their students.

We aren't Hollywood directors or movie stars. Our students aren't expecting to see the next *Avengers* movie in their college courses. We're teachers and students who are seeking ways to build real connections in service of our humanity and the learning process. The most important part of any educational video is that it supports those connections.

Further, I would argue that since many of us work with new-traditional students who are seeking validation of their role as a college student (see tip 25), a hyperproduced video like the ones described previously could actually be an obstacle to the learning process. My videos are real. They are human. They show me making mistakes and carrying on. They deconstruct hierarchies in the classroom, rather than reinforcing them.

Leave Hollywood to Hollywood. Let's focus instead on building human connections.

TIP 37: SATISFICE

◀◀ I ▶▶

Nope, that's not a typo. The title of this tip is "Satisfice," and it's a strategy to help you decide what kinds of videos are best for you, the focus of this section. What is satisficing, and how can it help you make awesome educational videos?

Satisficing is a concept from the field of decision-making theory, developed in the 1950s by a theorist named Herbert Simon (1956). The theory argues that we should make decisions by choosing a path that will provide adequate results. You know that old saying, "Shoot for the moon, for even if you fall short, you'll land among the stars"? Well, if you follow the method of satisficing, you're not going to do that. You'll shoot for the tallest tree in your backyard instead. Still pretty tall. Still a great view up there. Gets the job done.

Now I know that some of you might be questioning this approach. I can respect that. We live in a culture that tells us that 100% is not enough. The goal is 110%. What is that? How can anyone give more than 100%? I'm not sure that anyone knows, but a lot of us are trying and burning ourselves out in the process.

I think that being a mom has helped me get more comfortable with satisficing. There are millions of things that our world tells me that I'm supposed to do to be a great mom: Most of them are easily accessed on Pinterest. I don't bake theme cakes for my son's birthday. I don't dress him like a child model. I don't provide him with a plate of crudité when he gets home from school. I love him with my whole heart and other than that, I do my best, which is good enough.

This sage advice presents another interpretation of satisficing: Don't let perfection be the enemy of good. I sense that one of the biggest reasons that teachers don't create videos is the devil that is perfectionism. You know that your videos won't be perfect, so you don't make *any* videos. Whom does that serve?

I make imperfect, adequate videos that my students love and that I enjoy creating, using the time that I have available. If someone else's idea of what a perfect educational video should be is blocking you from getting started, stop trying to satisfy them and start satisficing yourself.

Reference

Simon, H. A. (1956). Rational choice and the structure of the environment. *Psychological Review, 63*(2), 129–138.

TIP 38: CREATE A TALKING HEAD VIDEO

◀◀ ❙ ▶▶

Take a moment to download and listen to any song from the Talking Heads to enjoy while reading this tip. "Burning Down the House" is one of my favorites (Talking Heads, 1983). Now, with a little musical inspiration under your belt, let's take a closer look at one of my favorite types of videos: the talking head video, also known as a headshot video. Sadly, we aren't going to be making a cool 1980s video that will air on MTV. We will, however, be creating an awesome educational video that will help you build sound relationships with your students.

For many of you, headshot videos are going to be your best bet in terms of simplicity and sustainability. I find this to be the easiest type of video to create, and it takes very little time to do it well (not perfectly, but well). That said, I want to be very clear that for those of you who are uncomfortable on camera (see Section Nine), the idea that this is the easiest type of video might have you scratching your head. At this stage of the process, we're not making any videos, so take a breath and keep reading for now. I want you to get a feel for all of your options, and then you can decide what types of videos will work best for you.

A headshot video can be recorded most efficiently by using the built-in webcam that is included on most computers. If you don't have a built-in webcam, a plug-in webcam that will clip to the top of your computer will work just as well and can be purchased for as little as $20. Finally, almost every adult I know, for better or worse, owns and uses a smartphone with a camera that can be used to record a talking head video.

This type of video will consist of a recording of you talking to your students. It's most typically filmed with you seated, capturing your upper half. Most teachers that I know, myself included, record these in their offices with a professional background behind them (see tip 53). You'll push record and start talking. Other than the possibility of some on-camera-induced nerves, this is as simple as it gets for most teachers. In my video-creation process, I tend to either make headshot videos or a combination of a headshot video with a screencast (see tip 41).

The benefit of the headshot video is that the focus is on you and your humanity without any other images for students to consider. If you're engaging—and I know that you will be, because you're going to learn how to develop your on-camera personality in Section Seven—you will capture your students' attention and have the chance to share a story, valuable content, or to inspire your students to greatness. These types of videos are both simple and powerful.

Take a moment to note your initial reaction to being on camera. We'll revisit those feelings throughout this book, because many of the faculty I've worked with have mixed feelings about it. For now, just notice. You'll have ample time to process this decision, and I'll give you lots of strategies, no matter the approach that you choose.

Reference

Talking Heads. (1983). Burning down the house. On *Speaking in tongues* [album]. Sire.

TIP 39: WEBCAM OR PHONE?

◀◀ ❙ ▶▶

In my experience, faculty who currently incorporate videos into their teaching are split about 50/50 in whether they create their videos using the webcams on their computers or their smartphones. There are no wrong answers here; instead, let's weigh the pros and cons of each choice. I would also encourage you to try each type of video a couple of times before you decide what works best for you. You'll have a chance to create several practice videos in Section Twelve, and I encourage you to try some on your computer and some on your phone.

As an initial step, it's worth comparing the quality of your webcam's and phone's cameras. For example, my trusty 2012 Mac's built-in webcam is 720p, and my iPhone 8's forward-facing camera is equipped for 1080p HD video recording (a higher number means better resolution on your videos). In short, my phone's camera quality is slightly better than my webcam's. Videos I record there will be a bit crisper. For some, the desire for a sharp-looking video will be paramount in their decision-making process. Again, the best method here is to try both types of videos and compare the experience and outcome.

There are other factors to consider when comparing your computer webcam to your phone. For example, if video quality is important to you, some folks will purchase an external webcam with higher quality resolution to use with their computer. You can buy a webcam with 1080p for around $50. That would allow you the same level of quality as your phone.

Next, think about whether or not you like to speak with your hands. I do. For me, holding my phone while filming feels awkward. I'm much more comfortable talking into my laptop's webcam. Of course, you do have the option of purchasing a mini-tripod for your phone, which would allow you to record with it while using your hands.

In the spirit of simplicity, though, I'm hesitant to tack on too many extra elements. I record most of my videos for my students using my computer. I've got a system in place that works, and it doesn't require any additional setup. There was a period of a few years where I used a much more complex system that included a tripod and a huge, white backdrop. It became so stressful that I found myself dreading making a video. While those videos might have been a bit more visually appealing, if I was going to avoid making them, that visual appeal was worthless.

Try a couple of practice videos (see Section Twelve) on your computer and phone. Notice how each feels while you're recording. Then, view the finished videos. Which is better quality? Is the difference very noticeable? Weigh your comfort level while making the video with the outcome, remembering that our goal isn't perfect, but good.

Finally, know that you aren't signing up for a lifetime commitment when you make this decision. It's fine to use your computer's webcam now and then switch to your phone later, or vice versa. It's also entirely possible that some new technology will arrive that we'll want to integrate into our videos in the future. Go with whichever choice seems the most simple and sustainable, knowing that it's normal for your system to evolve with time.

Position your smartphone's camera over Figure 39.1 to view a video about this tip.

Figure 39.1. Video: *Webcam or Phone?*

Note. Retrieved from https://youtu.be/xExHY6758XA

TIP 40: MEET YOUR NEW BEST FRIEND

Screencasts

◄◄ I ►►

I'm so excited to share this tip with you, because I sense that a lot of people don't realize that screencasts are an awesome, simple, and sustainable option for their educational videos. In my early teaching days, I spent a lot of time with advanced video creators who would toss around the names of fancy, expensive screencasting software programs. *I'll never figure out how to make a screencast,* I thought. I am here to tell you that screencasts are a tremendous teaching tool that you can create in less than 15 minutes, for free.

Let's start by explaining what a screencast is in a bit more detail. A screencast is a recording of your screen. Right now, if I were to do a screencast of my screen, it would capture me typing into this Word document. Screencasts most typically include audio as well, so that you can record your speech while explaining whatever is happening on your screen. In my online teaching, I often record myself demonstrating how to navigate a learning management system (LMS) for new students, or I'll pull up directions for an upcoming assignment on my screen and talk students through it. Many instructors will create a slide deck using PowerPoint, for example, and record a lecture using those slides.

Screencasts consist of a recording of what is on your screen accompanied by your audio. No webcam recording (i.e., talking head) is required. Screencasts without my talking head are definitely part of my video creation process, especially when I have a head cold (i.e., Rudolph the Red-Nosed Reindeer). In this approach, students will gain access to a view of your screen and your voice, which is a nice change of pace from explaining things solely in writing. The visual aspect of the screencast can be helpful to many students, and you can engage them with the power of your voice. Additionally, one could argue that for certain content, showing our talking head could be distracting and push on the limits of students' cognitive load.

As always, think carefully about your instructional goals, your time, and your comfort with being on camera. In many cases, when you weigh those factors, a screencast with audio only will be the ideal choice.

This tip covered the basics of why you might choose to use a screencast. Learn more about the practical steps toward recording a screencast in Tip 76: Try Screencasts With Audio Only and in Tip 83: Try This Simple and Sustainable Recording and Sharing Tool. You can also find an example of a screencast by following the link in Figure 77.1.

TIP 41: COMBINE SCREENCASTS WITH TALKING HEADS

◀◀ I ▶▶

Of all the different types of videos that I create, what I'm about to introduce you to in this tip is my favorite by far. You read about talking head (or headshot) videos in tip 38 and about screencasts in tip 40. Now, we'll explore how you can combine these two elements.

A headshot video lets you show students who you are and remind them that you're a real person with a beating heart, not a robot. Screencasts allow you to show students various elements on your screen, such as pages from your course within a learning management system. When you combine these two elements, you'll typically have a large section focused on the screencast element with a small thumbnail video that captures your headshot. Students get the best of both worlds.

You might be wondering why we'd combine these two elements. For example, if you are doing a screencast of a slide deck with an audio lecture, why bother including the headshot? The content is in front of them, so why do they need to see you?

I wish there were a mountain handy, so I could climb it and shout this from its peak: The relationships that we build with our students are critical to the teaching and learning experience. It's easy to fall into the trap of focusing solely on content, but I beg of you to always start with the relationship. Everything we know about the brain tells us that we humans are social animals (Lieberman, 2013) who learn best when our brains are swimming in the chemicals that are born of positive experiences (Whitman & Kelleher, 2016).

When explaining course content, ideas, or assignments to students via screencasts, the most humanizing, engaging, connecting choice is to add a headshot video as well. You might choose not to do this for a variety of reasons (see Section Nine), but to prioritize content over relationships shouldn't be one of those reasons.

Now that we understand the reasons behind using this type of video, a word on logistics: I'll identify my preferred method for creating screencasts with headshots in Section Ten. Read Tip 83: Try This Simple and Sustainable Recording and Sharing Tool to get started. If you'd like to see an example of a screencast with a headshot video, follow the link in Figure 85.1. This will show you an example of a video that I created using this method.

No matter what software you choose to use, be mindful of where you place the thumbnail of your headshot during your recording. If you are reviewing a grading rubric, for example, you don't want the thumbnail to cover the rubric. Other than that small concern, this is a very straightforward type of video to create and easy for you to sustain as part of your teaching practice.

References

Lieberman, M. D. (2013). *Social: Why our brains are wired to connect.* New York, NY: Broadway Books.

Whitman, G., & Kelleher, I. (2016). *Neuroteach: Brain science and the future of education.* Lanham, MD: Rowman & Littlefield.

SECTION FIVE

VIDEO TIMING AND COURSE PLACEMENT

How often will you share videos with your students? Will you focus on sharing videos early in the course, perhaps during the first week, or at the end of the course to end on a strong note? Where will you place the videos within the course so that they are most accessible to your students and make sense in terms of your overall course design?

Some tips in this section will be applicable to both online courses and flipped learning. Flipped learning is a relatively new teaching approach that has taken off in the last decade. Land-based teachers use flipped learning to shift their lectures outside of the classroom so that in-class time can be more effective and engaging. For those of you wishing to use videos to complement your work in your land-based courses, you'll find these tips helpful. Are you ready for a full flip, or do you want to begin slowly by flipping one class at a time? Which content is most conducive to a flipped learning model?

All of these are questions that you'll have a chance to consider in this section. As you read, don't get too caught up in finding the perfect timing and placement for your courses. Use this information to develop a plan and know that all great designs go through a process of revision. Start where you are, use your tools, and decide what will work best for your upcoming classes, knowing that you can adapt this approach in the future as needed.

TIP 42: USE COURSE
ANNOUNCEMENTS

◀◀ ❙ ▶▶

If you are teaching online, you're probably using some form of course announcements that you manage through your learning management system (LMS). Course announcements are a great way to communicate with our students, and in every LMS I've used, you can create announcements ahead of time and release them at a later date. If you aren't teaching fully online, chances are that you have access to an online course shell that supports your land-based teaching, making course announcements an excellent tool for offline or hybrid courses as well.

Some LMSs will allow you to record videos directly into the announcement. In other cases, your best bet is to upload your video to YouTube and either share the link or embed the video (see tip 81) within the course announcement. Consider which option will be the simplest and most sustainable for you.

Most online instructors I know release at least a couple of course announcements each week, sometimes more. You'll want to balance using this opportunity to connect with your students with overloading them. In general, an initial announcement at the start of the week and a wrap-up announcement at the end of the week is a great place to start. Will you include a video in both your opening and closing announcements? Again, you'll want to weigh the value of connection against what we know about cognitive load, which is that too much information at once is detrimental for learning. Two videos per week might be too much, not enough, or just right. Think about your students, your course content, and your own time when making that decision. I feel that one video per week is ideal.

One of the great benefits of placing your videos within your course announcements is that it's very easy to plan these out ahead of time. In a 15-week course, you could create 15 videos and embed them in the opening announcement for each week. Since you're going to create videos that are easily reusable from term to term (see tip 63), you can then copy these announcements into future sections. This is a simple and sustainable system that will engage students and avoid overwhelming them.

Take a moment to reflect on how you currently use announcements in your teaching. Would this be the ideal place in your course to share videos? If so, how often would you like to include a video? Every week? Once every few weeks? Keep the model of simplicity and sustainability in mind while also recognizing that there's no one-size-fits-all answer; decide what works best for you in your teaching.

TIP 43: INCLUDE VIDEOS IN E-MAILS

◀◀ I ▶▶

Another way that you can share videos with students is through e-mails. Let's a moment to recognize that in some learning management systems (LMSs), course announcements and e-mails are intertwined. You might have the option to post a course announcement that is then pushed through to students' e-mails. In that case, you can easily share videos through both announcements and e-mails with one click.

In other LMSs, you might not have this option. You also might not feel that course announcements are the best place for you to share videos with your students. In that case, sharing via e-mail is another option. Note that in this tip, I'm talking about bulk e-mails to your entire class. We'll learn more about using videos with individual students in tip 47.

You might have easy access to a class e-mail list in your LMS, or maybe you keep an e-mail list of your own creation (more likely if you teach in a traditional format). You can copy your video's URL from YouTube (see tip 81) and include it in the e-mail, or you can use the embed code to embed the video in the e-mail.

If you send e-mails to students on a consistent schedule (perhaps on Monday of each week), you might wish to also be consistent about including a video in that e-mail. If you're more likely to send e-mails on the fly, that's fine too. If that's the case, identify the main topic of the e-mail and consider if a video could complement your message. A quick "just saying hello" type video would also work on occasion. I also make sure to include video verbiage in the subject line of the e-mail, hoping to catch students' attention (e.g., "Video Tutorial Inside!").

Using e-mail is a bit less organized than including regular videos in your course announcements. If you're more of a free spirit in your teaching and like to go with the flow, this option might feel more intuitive to you. That's the beauty of video: Within this simple and sustainable model, you have many options to select from that will work with your personality and teaching style.

Do you send e-mails to your class? If so, how would adding either occasional or consistent videos to those e-mails work for you and your students?

TIP 44: COMPLEMENT COURSE DISCUSSIONS

◀◀ I ▶▶

Another place that you might want to share your videos is within online course discussions. Many online courses use weekly discussions, so if you're looking to be consistent with sharing videos, posting them weekly in the discussion makes a lot of sense.

I would recommend that you consider the content of your videos and to what extent they align with the discussion topic. Unrelated topics could confuse students. For example, if the weekly discussion is on a short story and you post a video about an assignment on a different topic that's approaching in two weeks, that isn't the best fit. However, if the video is focused on how students can write an exceptional post about the short story, placing that within the discussion area makes more sense.

Of the various ways that I share videos with students, this is the least likely place that I use videos in my teaching. That said, if you've identified improving the engagement level in the discussion as a significant focus of your teaching, using videos here is in perfect alignment with your goals.

If you choose to share videos that align with the discussion, your learning management system (LMS) might offer the option to record a video directly into your discussion post. Consider, however, if you'll be able to easily copy this video into future courses. If not, posting the video into YouTube (see tip 81) and then sharing the URL or embedding the video into a discussion post is a better option.

Is boosting student success and learning in the course discussion one of your teaching goals? Do you plan to share videos that are in alignment with course discussion topics? If so, placing videos in the discussion is a great starting point for you.

TIP 45: LOCATE VIDEOS WITHIN COURSE CONTENT

◄◄ ▮ ►►

Most of us have an organized system for our online course content. Perhaps you organize your content into chapters, themes, weeks, or modules. A system like this is essential to help lessen the demands on our students' cognitive load and to make it very clear how they should navigate the course.

No matter how your course is organized, you might want to place your videos within your course content. For example, you could include an introductory video for each week of the course within the weekly folder. I've done this and have seen it used by many others. It's a very simple strategy, and it's a nice way to get students motivated for the upcoming week.

Typically, this type of video introduces the focus of the week and helps students see how that focus relates to the broader goals of the course. For example, if you are teaching an anatomy and physiology course and this week's focus is the autonomic nervous system, you might refer back to the broader purpose of the course, which is to teach students about the biology and function of the human body.

Another approach would be a short video lecture on the week's topic. Information on creating instructionally sound lectures is found in Section Eight. Your weekly folder of content could include a video lecture, discussion, and links to interactive or engaging external content.

Finally, if you have any assignments in that section of the course, your video could review the assignment with students in detail and offer them some helpful tips. Make sure that students have access to the assignment video tutorial in plenty of time to make use of it when they're working on the assignment. For example, if there's a major assignment that students should be working on two weeks in advance of the assignment deadline, you might wish to put the video tutorial in the prior week's folder of content. Of course, in all of our videos, regardless of the specific focus, we always have the chance to humanize ourselves in the video. Keep that intention front and center.

If you're going to choose this placement for your video, consider how many videos you plan to create. Ideally, for the sake of consistency, you would add a video to each section of the course. For example, if your course is divided into 10 chapters or folders, you would include a video in each chapter's content.

That said, you could consider videos for each section as a long-term goal and work on adding 1 video to 1 chapter as a starting point. Next term, you could add 1 or 2 more. Rome wasn't built in a day, and progress beats perfection every time. Some of you might have the time and energy to bang out 10 videos in a row before the start of your next term. I've done that before, and you can do it in a few hours. You might not want to talk to anyone for a few days after you finish, but it's definitely feasible. If that sounds like too much for you, not to worry. Start by adding 1 video to the first content section of your course. You can even tell your students in an e-mail or course announcement that you are working on adding more videos to the course, you are starting with a single video, and you'd love their feedback on that video.

How do you organize your course content? Would placing videos into the course content be a good starting point on your video creation journey?

TIP 46: TRY ON-THE-FLY VIDEOS

◀◀ ❙ ▶▶

In this section's previous tips, I encouraged you to find a method to share videos consistently with your students, whether through course announcements, e-mail, discussions, or course content. Most of us would agree that organization and consistency make for a stronger classroom learning experience, whether we're teaching online or land-based courses. I've found that being organized helps my students and me. I'm a big fan of structure.

In this tip, however, we're going to throw organization and structure out the window. Why not? I'm a believer that we should be a bit more both/and

and a lot less either/or in our thinking about education and the world. Let's throw caution to the wind and dance in the paradox. Can you be organized in your timing and placement of videos *and* also share them on the fly? Yes.

Let's assume that you've decided on a method for sharing 1 or more videos with your students consistently. For example, you are going to send out videos with your weekly course announcements in your 15-week course. This is a great plan.

With this plan in place, you begin teaching and reach week 4, when all hell breaks loose. You are getting e-mails every 30 minutes from students who are confused about the upcoming midterm paper. Or, you review your students' recent quiz grades and realize that no one in the course understands a critical course concept. What to do?

Make a video. Without a plan, without attention to consistency, without a second thought, turn on your webcam or smartphone and start recording. Create a video on the fly to address an unexpected and pressing need. We call this "a teachable moment," and they are one of the best parts of teaching. They keep us on our toes and challenge us to return to the beginner's mind, how we thought before we knew everything under the sun about our field of study. This type of ad hoc video might not be part of your carefully laid video creation plans, but it can be an excellent teaching tool to support student learning.

TIP 47: SHARE VIDEOS WITH INDIVIDUAL STUDENTS

◄◄ I ►►

This book is based on a model aimed at helping you do your very best teaching while also maintaining your sanity in our hectic world. Teachers at all levels are often pulled in many directions and seem to wear an increasing number of hats in the workplace. The goal of videos is not to add more to your plate, but to help you create a system that will save you time in the long run. It's essential to keep that in mind as you read this next tip. For some of you, the suggestion to create videos for individual students will be simple and sustainable. For others, this might be too much. Take what you need from this tip and leave the rest.

One of the ways that you might wish to use videos in your teaching is to create a short video for an individual student. I have used this option when a student is stuck and completely lost in terms of navigating some element of the course. Once a few e-mails have gone back and forth, it's sometimes much easier to show the student what they need to do rather than writing out 15 steps in an e-mail. I think it's a lot easier for the students, too.

I rarely create this type of video and rely on the more consistent approach detailed in the earlier tips in this section. I reserve the individual video option for more extreme situations when I'm dealing with a student who is new to online learning and who is getting frustrated trying to figure out next steps, typically around course navigation. I can create a quick screencast video for the student, demonstrating the appropriate steps, and we can both move on.

Even though I'm emphasizing that this is not going to be a simple and sustainable solution for all of you, when I have taken the time to create a personalized video for students, they are incredibly, effusively grateful for that attention to their needs. While you might not choose this option often, it's worth trying once to test the waters. You might find that the student reactions motivate you to want to incorporate these types of videos into your video creation process.

TIP 48: USE VIDEOS IN GRADED FEEDBACK

◀◀ I ▶▶

In this tip, I'll share how to use videos as part of your graded feedback to students. I've tried this before, and I've found that it's very time-consuming, and the payoff in how students received it wasn't worth the cost. However, one of the guiding principles of this book is that you know your teaching and your students best. This tip might be a hit for you.

Providing specific and actionable feedback to students on their assignments is an essential part of the teaching and learning process. Many of us are already doing this in written form, and others are likely using grading rubrics to support our students' learning experiences. Adding some video feedback might be an additional strategy that you'll want to explore.

How can you use videos in your graded feedback? To start, you'll want to decide if there are common themes that might warrant a video that you could share with all students in your feedback. For example, if you're going to remind all students that they should apply your suggested feedback and submit a revision of their assignment within one week, you could create a video about that process and the reason behind it to share with all students. In that case, you would write personalized feedback to students in a grading rubric or whatever system you use, and then you could provide some general feedback to all students, linking to your video.

Another option is to create personalized video feedback for individual students. There are a few ways to approach this. If you have the time, you could create videos for all students. I am going to venture a guess that most of you don't have that kind of time. Another approach would be to create videos for the students who appear to be struggling the most, or those who don't seem to have applied your previous feedback. In short, you triage your use of videos to reach the students most in need of additional intervention. You could also aim to give all your students at least one personalized video over the term. You could create a few videos per week and cycle through all your students.

Using videos for graded feedback is one of the more time-intensive suggestions in this book. If this doesn't seem like a priority for you, set this aside. If, however, you've been looking for a creative way to improve your graded feedback to students, videos might be a great addition to your teaching toolbox.

TIP 49: FLIP YOUR LAND-BASED COURSE

◀◀ I ▶▶

Flipped learning is an approach used when teaching primarily land-based courses. In a land-based course, it's still quite common for the primary teaching activity to be a lecture. Students are then assigned other homework activities to do on their own time outside of class. That model is switched in a flipped classroom. One of the most typical ways to flip a class is to record video lectures that students will watch on their own, in advance of coming to class. Then, class time is devoted to interactive activities that apply the lecture's concepts. Since lectures are often very passive, why not have students complete those outside of class?

Many of you might be teaching traditional classes that can benefit from videos through this model of flipped learning. I know teachers get very excited about flipping their courses, but when the idea of recording videos arises, you can hear the sound of tires screeching to a halt. *I want to try flipping my class*, you might be thinking, *But I'm scared to try videos.*

I taught a traditional course in the very early days of the flipped classroom movement. In alignment with the model of this book and my video creation philosophy, I kept it simple. I didn't try to flip my entire course for the whole semester; I tried flipping one class period at a time. Instead of viewing flipping as a huge endeavor that I was going to force myself to develop, I looked at it as an experiment. *Let me try flipping this one class and see how it goes*, I thought.

If you have your course fully developed, attempting to flip that entire course is going to be time-consuming. If you're game for a big summer project, go for it. However, if you want to take a slower approach, try flipping one or two of your lessons. Create a video that students will view before class and then take advantage of the in-person class time to do fun, engaging, interactive activities that give students hands-on practice to explore the course concepts.

If you want to flip, don't let your fears about making videos stand in your way. By keeping it simple and sustainable, you can easily pursue your flipping goals.

Position your smartphone's camera over Figure 49.1 to view a video about this tip.

Figure 49.1. Video: *Flip Your Land-Based Course.*

Note. Retrieved from https://youtu.be/Mc2tyTmz21Q

TIP 50: USE VIDEOS FOR CANCELED CLASSES

◄◄ I ►►

How many days of your land-based course did students miss last term due to snow days? Forget just snow days. I'm sure some of you have had ice days; fire days; flood days; and, sadly, a variety of canceled classes due to disaster recovery or other emergencies. There were also likely days when you canceled class due to your own illness or travel.

One of the most common challenges faculty share is that it feels almost impossible to fit the amount of content they need to teach into the time allotted to them. When a day or two is missed, it can leave us scrambling and throw off the rhythm of the entire course. One way to keep students on track is to offer online videos in place of a canceled land-based class.

To be clear, in most cases, this works best when you have some advance notice. For example, if you know that you'll be traveling to a conference on March 18th, you can note this in the syllabus as a "video day" and record the video ahead of time. You might combine this with some activities like discussion work or self-reflection.

What about unanticipated days off? Your options here will vary. If you are down for the count with the flu, you're probably not going to make a video. If you've just got a mild cold, you might feel that it's worth it to record a quick screencast (your red nose might not feel like being on camera) to help students stay on track.

I would suggest having a plan for canceled class days written into your syllabus. Tell students where they can receive notifications about cancellations and let them know to check their e-mail by noon (or whatever time) of that day to access information about videos or other work. If you typically teach from 1:00 p.m. to 2:30 p.m., you might provide students with an equivalent amount of work in the form of readings, activities, and videos. It is worth consulting with your supervisor to inquire about any policies at your institution around requiring online work for a canceled class.

You'll also want to keep in mind that in extreme weather scenarios, some students might lose access to the Internet, sometimes for days. You could lose access as well. If you're going to ask your students to complete missing work online, you should also be reasonably available to answer any questions about that work.

In the twenty-first century, it seems evident to me that when we can't meet in person, we would complete that work online. With nearly universal access to the Internet, why wouldn't we stay on track for our goals by using technology? While there are certainly going to be exceptions to this rule, creating videos to meet course deadlines and goals on days when classes are canceled seems to be an efficient use of technology to support our pedagogical goals.

TIP 51: INCORPORATE VIDEOS INTO MIDTERM AND FINAL REVIEWS

◀◀ ▌ ▶▶

In both online and traditional classrooms, videos can complement any review sessions that you offer for midterms or finals. One of the things that we know about how the brain learns best is that spaced repetition is ideal for both short-term and long-term retention. There are a lot of great studies about the ideal spacing between study sessions; in general, it's better to break up study across a period of days rather than to cram (Weinstein & Smith, 2016). Instead of one huge review session, could it benefit your students to offer spaced review through some online videos?

A review video could consist of you highlighting the type of test that students can expect (essay, multiple choice, etc.) and discussing suggested study strategies. Then, you could use class time to focus on specific content. Another option would be to cover key material in the video and then repeat that review in a later class. The goal here is to hit students' brains with test information on multiple occasions rather than in one fell swoop. If you're teaching online, you can e-mail review videos to students over a period of a few days leading up to an exam.

Think about the review videos you create as being a way to prime the pump. They will activate students' prior knowledge of the topic. One way to do this is to tell students that you are going to pose questions in the video and ask them to write down their responses. Students should bring these answers to the next in-person class, where they will then work in groups. Have students compare their answers, and then review as a large group. For online courses, ask students to talk about their answers in the course discussion.

There are several ways to use video for review sessions, so focus on what we know about student learning and be creative. The old model of one review session in the class immediately prior to the exam is outdated. It's time to build in additional sessions to capitalize on our knowledge of how the brain learns best.

Reference

Weinstein, Y., & Smith, M. (2016). Learn how to study using . . . spaced practice. *The Learning Scientists*. Retrieved from http://www.learningscientists.org/blog/2016/7/21-1

SECTION SIX

SETTING THE STAGE

A little bit of preparation can go a long way. The tips in this section will help you prepare to create awesome instructional videos. In keeping with the simple and sustainable model, you'll find a series of quick tips that anyone can do, regardless of experience level. By taking just a bit of time to set the stage for your videos, I think you'll find that they are of better quality, and the process will be less stressful and more enjoyable.

Like anything else in life, the more you do this work, the better you'll get at it. At first, you might want to have your copy of this book handy when you start creating videos. Over time, your preparation process will become intuitive. Today, when I'm ready to create a video, I don't need to think about it; I just do it. The neural pathways that I've built over the years take over, and that will happen for you too.

After reading this section, you'll feel much more confident about the actual recording process, because you'll have taken the appropriate steps to create a setting that will lead to high-quality videos. Start reading, and prepare to set the stage for the excellent work that you'll do for yourself and your students.

TIP 52: FIND DECENT LIGHTING

◀◀ I ▶▶

I've seen some dark videos, and I'm not talking about their themes; I'm talking about their lighting. Some of the educational videos that I've seen look like someone is auditioning for a horror movie. You don't need professional lighting to create a great video, but you do need decent lighting.

Before I give you some tips on lighting, I want to share a quick story. Several years ago, I felt like I wanted to improve my videos and take them to some imagined next level. I spent several hundred dollars on a lighting set that I bought online. It came in a huge black bag that looked like I could've fit a body in it. There were lights, umbrellas, a big white screen, and lots of adjustable poles. I talked my husband into emptying the guest room in our house so that I could set up my own production studio. I also recruited him to help me figure out where to place the various elements of my lighting system, spending hours with me as we experimented with different placements.

Each time I wanted to create a video, I'd find myself spending an hour getting the setup to work. Then, guests came to visit. I packed it all away to make room for the air mattress, but when it came time to put the system back in place, I didn't have the energy. Today, the body bag is sitting somewhere in our basement's crawl space.

Now, I record next to a window that offers solid natural light. I turn on the other lights in the room, and I get down to business. The lighting isn't going to win me any awards, but it's of sufficient quality for the types of videos that I create. It gets the job done.

You don't need to buy any special lighting. However, take some time to consider if you need to bring in some additional floor lamps to your recording space. If possible, record next to a window to capture some natural light. With these few simple adjustments, your videos will go from horror to upbeat feel-good flick in no time.

TIP 53: TAKE A LOOK BEHIND YOU

◀◀ I ▶▶

I mentioned in tip 52 that I once invested in a lighting system that came with a large white screen that I placed behind me when filming. The time and energy that it took to open and collapse it were not sustainable for me. Today, I record most of my videos in a small office space that I have set up in the family room in our house. In my videos, you'll see me sitting in front of our bookshelves: nothing fancy, but still professional.

I want you to take a moment to imagine a spectrum with the word *professional* at one end and *personal* at the other (a false dichotomy, but useful for this exercise). Your background, and your videos in general, should fall somewhere in between. In hindsight, I now see that a completely plain white background was boring and impersonal. However, I've seen some faculty create videos in their bedrooms with a shot of their beds behind them: nope, way too personal.

It's great to have some visuals behind you that add a human touch. Students who watch your videos will see some of your favorite books or a picture. You could have some motivational quotes or anything that you collect in your background shot. I wouldn't recommend that it be too cluttered or busy, but a few significant items will help remind students that you are a human being with interests, feelings, and a personality. This will serve to further support the student–teacher relationship.

One other consideration is to be mindful of leaving out any sensitive or confidential information that could be picked up in your shot. An example of this would be a student roster with student ID numbers or your last credit card statement.

Where are you planning to record your videos? What will be behind you? Does it balance personality with professionalism?

Position your smartphone's camera over Figure 53.1 to view a video about this tip.

Figure 53.1. Video: *Take a Look Behind You.*

Note. Retrieved from https://youtu.be/ZPCq4Ft7R9M

TIP 54: KEEP THE CAMERA LENS LEVEL WITH YOUR FACE

◀◀ I ▶▶

Another big issue that I see in videos is camera placement. This is a 10-second fix, so there's no reason to ignore it.

If your camera is positioned too low, it's going to focus on the bottom of your chin. An online friend of mine who makes videos for his students recently referred to this as "catching chin." I don't care if you're a supermodel; that's no one's best look. I want my students to focus on my ideas, not the insides of my nostrils.

Alternatively, if the camera is placed too high, you're going to be looking up at it. This doesn't look professional, and as a certified yoga teacher who has studied arthritis and chronic pain, I can tell you that it could potentially hurt your neck over time. We don't want our videos to send us to the chiropractor. I also don't love the look of a camera that's placed at an angle to the right or left and, and this could also cause neck strain over time. These are my personal preferences, so I encourage you to play around with them a bit and see which camera placement you like best.

I suggest that you place your camera at eye level and directly in front of you. Since most of you will be using the webcam that's built into your computer, you might need to move your screen or monitor. I sometimes film on a laptop that I boost to eye level by placing it on two yoga blocks. There are also computer stands built explicitly for this purpose that you can purchase. For a price comparison, my yoga blocks probably cost me about eight dollars each. When I record on my desktop, since the screen is bigger, no adjustments are needed.

If you are using an external webcam, you'll want to play around with placement until you find the best optics for your videos. Another online friend of mine told me that her external webcam came with a mini-tripod that she found particularly delightful. The many benefits of being an online educator!

If you film on your smartphone, the same rules apply. Hold the phone at eye level, or, if you're using a tripod (both small and large tripods are available), adjust accordingly. Keep in mind that if you're going to be filming for more than a couple of minutes and plan to hold your smartphone, you might end up creating a very bumpy video. Holding your phone for quick, on-the-fly videos will work just fine. If you're going to be filming for more than two or three minutes, I'd recommend a smartphone tripod.

Like all the tips in this book, camera lens location is something that you'll want to play with until you figure out the best placement for you. Try a few different approaches and then decide on the one that looks the best and is comfortable for you. The goal here is to find a camera angle that results in a great video and allows you to feel confident when filming.

TIP 55: USE A MICROPHONE

◄◄ I ►►

Before you start to worry that you're going to waste hours of your life researching microphones online, let me cut to the chase very quickly: In our simple and sustainable video creation system, basic earbuds with a built-in microphone are all that you need to produce acceptable audio for your videos. In case you didn't realize it, the earbuds that probably came with your smartphone have a little microphone built into the cord. On my set, it's part of the piece that allows me to adjust the volume. Cool, right?

In my early video creation days, I didn't use any microphone. As I dove deeper into the world of video, I heard a common refrain: The easiest way to boost a video's quality is to improve its audio. If you aren't using a microphone, your voice gets a bit lost, and you're much more likely to pick up background noise. At the time, I went ahead and bought a headset like sportscasters wear in the booth when calling games. It had big headphones that went over my ears and a microphone that jutted out in front of my mouth. It worked well, but it took up more space on my desk than I liked, and I slowly gravitated toward earbuds. Simplify!

If you want to play around with this tip, open the voice memo app on your phone and create two recordings: In the first, don't use a mic. In the second, use your earbuds. You'll likely notice a slight improvement in sound with the earbuds. This is a simple, affordable (free if you already own earbuds) strategy that can boost the quality of your videos in the time that it takes to plug the earbuds into your computer or to fight your teenager for them.

TIP 56: WILL YOU BRUSH YOUR HAIR?

◀◀ I ▶▶

Recently, I saw an online educator share a video that she'd made for her students on Twitter. In the video, she wore a very stylish black fedora. First off, I love people who wear cool hats. They're really some of the best people. Second, I thought this was the perfect example of the choices that we'll need to make as human beings and professionals when recording our videos.

I want to clarify here that this tip is not about vanity or meeting some external standard of beauty. I'm discussing appearance in the context of helping you create a system that will empower you to feel confident when being on camera. Some readers will feel confident after having just rolled out of bed; others will choose to take some time to primp a bit. The choice is yours, but it's a consideration worthy of your attention as you think through how you're going to make this system your own.

I work from home, so most days, the amount of time that I put into my appearance is minimal. However, when I record a video, I feel most comfortable when I've done some basic preparation in the form of a bit of makeup and blow-drying my hair. I don't feel comfortable or confident recording with a bare face and a wet bun wearing a t-shirt with holes in it. If I know that I'm going to be recording videos, I'll make the time to devote an extra 15 minutes to my appearance and put on a more professional shirt.

There are also some days when I feel like my students need a video from me, and I want to meet that need, but I don't have the energy to make myself more presentable. It happens. On those days, I turn to trusty tip 40: I make screencasts with audio only and no headshot recording. My problem is solved. I don't rely on that all the time, but I have learned that pressuring myself to do something that I'm just not up for is a motivation killer.

You'll need to decide how you want to handle your appearance when filming. If you work outside of the home and you already make time to put on your grown-up face and clothes, this will be less of a concern. You're already camera-ready. For those of you who work from home, you'll want to consider this question, in terms of not only what you are comfortable with but also time. If you want to put on some makeup and style your hair before filming, you've got to factor that into your video creation process. If you couldn't care less about how you look and think this tip is a bunch of hogwash, bravo. Proceed as you see fit.

TIP 57: REDUCE BACKGROUND NOISE

◄◄ I ►►

Thank goodness for my dog, Rocky, and his predecessor, Coco. If not for them, I wouldn't notice every time a truck drives past our house or a squirrel runs across the backyard. Coco, an English Springer Spaniel, was adept at notifying me with loud barking in response to any anomalies in the neighborhood. Rocky, a shih tzu, has happily inherited Coco's job and takes his work very seriously.

Life makes noise, especially if you are a pet owner or parent. While many of my videos have very little background noise, in others, you'll hear the sound of my dog barking. I used to curse, yell at my dog, and stop recording. Increasingly, I'm letting life happen in my videos. I'm much more likely now to smile and say, "There's Rocky, everyone, saying hello and making sure that you all know there's a leaf blowing across my yard." Rocky settles down, and I keep filming. If it were a major bark-a-thon, I'd start over. If it's only a few yaps, I keep going.

Certainly, do your best to reduce background noise, but know that sometimes it's out of our control. Attending to every sound in the environment and constantly restarting your videos is not sustainable. Do your best, but remember that perfection is the enemy of good.

Before you start filming, take a minute to notice and eliminate any additional background noise that might get picked up by the microphone. What sound do you have control over? In other words, if you have a space heater on in the background or your radiator clangs, turn it off or move rooms. Some of us, however, live in urban areas where noises like sirens and street construction are just part of daily life. I've listened to amazing podcasts by people with huge followings who have horns honking regularly in the background. Do your best to eliminate distracting background noise, but don't feel like you need to move to the country if you can't.

Kids will yell. Spouses will drop a pan ("Sorry, honey, were you filming?"). You'll forget to set your phone to do not disturb. Life will make noise. Do your best to reduce too many distracting noises, but know that it's often okay to carry on and use these noises as a talking point or humanizing element in your videos.

SECTION SEVEN

PRESENTATION TIPS

At this point in the book, you've laid a strong foundation for your video creation process. Now, it's time to push "record" and start making videos. Whatever your experience with videos or your comfort level, there's a solution for you in this section that will help you either make awesome instructional videos or improve the ones that you're already creating.

What I most want to highlight here is that our goal is not perfection. Perfection is an illusion, and I find that striving for it can result in videos that are grating and disengaging. Being human is where it's at, and that's the ultimate goal in these videos. That said, I'm always an advocate of balance. The tips in this section will help you create high-quality videos that look and sound great while also helping you connect with your students on a human level.

After reading this section, you'll have some simple and sustainable presentation skills to start creating your videos. I have been using all of these recommendations in my videos for a decade, and they have passed inspection from the many faculty that I've worked with in my career. I hope they will help you feel empowered in this process and that some of your misconceptions about what it takes to make a great video will fall away, releasing you from the pressure of perfectionism and inviting you into a fun, creative, and engaging video creation practice.

TIP 58: DON'T USE A SCRIPT

◄◄ I ►►

You're new to video, but you've decided to give it a shot. *I know*, you think, *I'll use a script so that I don't twist words or forget what I'm going to say.*

That plan makes sense, doesn't it? And the road to hell is paved with good intentions.

There is a small population of people who can read off a script and make it engaging for their audience: These people are known as professional broadcasters. With respect, if you are reading this book, you are probably not one of them. For most of us, if we use a script in our videos, it will be awkward. Our eyes will dart back and forth between the text and the camera. It will come off as uncomfortable and stiff. Your audience will quickly disengage. Something more interesting will catch their attention.

If you're worried about making mistakes, remember this: You're going to create educational videos meant to engage both you and your students; you're not on trial. You do not need to read a prepared statement that has been approved by your lawyer. Making mistakes is okay. In fact, it's preferable! Remember, one of the reasons that you're going to start creating videos is to humanize the online learning experience. What is more human? Someone reading off a script like an automaton or a person speaking from the heart?

When I first started filming my videos, I felt like they had to be perfect. What's a surefire recipe for misspeaking in a video? Insisting on perfection. I would push through take after take, exhausting myself in the process. Eventually, after a few semesters of this unsustainable approach, I surrendered. If I misspoke on a video, I'd correct myself and keep filming. If I'd forgotten to turn my phone off and a text vibrated in the background, I'd silence it and then remind my students why phones can be a distraction from learning. If my dog barked at the trash truck, I'd tilt the camera toward him and have him say hello to my students.

The sky didn't fall. I would argue that these mistakes made my videos even better because they made me more human.

Instead of using a script, jot down some general ideas that you'd like to cover in your video. Then, speak from the heart. Your videos will be better for it.

103

TIP 59: DON'T READ SLIDES

◀◀ ▐ ▶▶

One of my favorite educational memes has a picture of Morpheus (played by Laurence Fishburne) from the movie *The Matrix*, posing the question, "What if I told you that reading a PowerPoint aloud is not the same as teaching?" (Morpheus, n.d.). Once you ask this question, you'll never be the same again. You'll notice how often people read slide decks to an audience in classrooms, workshops, and professional trainings. I love presentation tools, but when misused, they can do more harm than good.

Design and presentation experts recommend that you drastically limit the amount of text on a slide (Reynolds, 2012). Indeed, some argue for no more than five words per slide. In addition, research out of the field of mind, brain, and education science has found that we don't listen as well when we are reading (Horvath, 2014). In other words, if there is a copious amount of text presented to us while someone is also speaking, our visual processing pathways will trump our auditory ones, meaning we'll focus on what we're reading and filter out what we're hearing. As teachers, that means that if we use a ton of text on a slide, our students' brains will focus on reading it, and they'll ignore everything we're saying.

Many of you will choose to create video lectures. This is a great idea if done well. However, if you create a screencast recording (tip 40) that captures text-heavy PowerPoint slides while you record an audio of your voice reading the slides to your students, you're going to not only ignore principles of brain science but also bore your students to tears (and anger Morpheus—never a good idea).

We'll learn more about how to integrate slide decks into our videos in Section Eight. For now, know that if you choose to create lectures that rely on slides, limit the amount of text on your slides to around 10 words. Use images when possible, and briefly describe those images for students with visual impairments. Video creation is often a starting point to reimagining your relationship to PowerPoint. As promised, once you start doing that work, you'll never be the same.

References

Horvath, J. C. (2014). The neuroscience of PowerPoint. *Mind, Brain, and Education, 8*(3), 137–142.

Morpheus [Digital image]. (n.d.). Retrieved from https://imgflip.com/i/46zvm

Reynolds, G. (2012). *Presentation Zen: Simple ideas on presentation design and delivery*. Berkeley, CA: New Riders.

TIP 60: MAKE EYE CONTACT

◀◀ I ▶▶

Making and maintaining eye contact is tough for some of us. As an introvert, I'm a little uncomfortable with it, and I tend to focus anywhere other than the person in front of me. I remember a few years ago when someone called me on it for the first time: "Why aren't you looking at me when I'm talking to you?" I hadn't fully realized that I did this until I was asked that question. Since then, I've tried to be a bit more aware of it and to at least make occasional eye contact when talking to someone, in recognition of this social norm.

In theory, keeping eye contact when creating online videos should be more accessible because we're not staring into the soul of another person, but rather a small black lens on our computer screen or smartphone. However, it takes focus to keep my eyes on the camera lens; it's not visually appealing, and it's small, so it tires out my eyes fairly quickly.

In addition, if I'm recording a talking head video, there's typically a small thumbnail video of that recording in the lower right side of my screen. The temptation is to stare at myself, which for me entails wondering if I should try a new haircut or noticing that my shirt looks a little wrinkly. Keeping our eyes off that little square and focused on the camera takes tremendous self-control.

I've seen some people cut an arrow out of a brightly colored sticky note and point it at their webcam as a way to help them make eye contact during their video. If you struggle to keep your eyes on the lens, give this a try. For me, the solution is practice, as well as observing the outcome of a video with poor eye contact, whether it's my own or someone else's. When I'm in the video's audience, there's an immediate disconnect when the person behind the screen isn't looking directly at me. It's distracting, and my sense of connection with that person is lost. Noticing that disconnect has been enough to help me maintain eye contact most of the time.

I also like to imagine my students on the other side of the camera. I'm just a human being, talking to a bunch of other human beings. I speak to my audience from my heart, and that motivates me to maintain eye contact. Keep practicing, and keep people in mind as you create your videos. Your eye contact might not be perfect at first, but with continued practice and self-observation, you'll soon stare into that small, black dot like an expert.

TIP 61: PERFECT YOUR POSTURE

◀◀ ❙ ▶▶

A few years ago, I attended a workshop called "Change Your Posture, Change Your Life" at the Kripalu Center for Yoga and Health. The presenter, Michaelle Edwards (2016), warned us on the first night that learning about posture was a little bit like being the kid in the movie *The Sixth Sense*. Remember him? "I see dead people . . ." (Shyamalan, 1999, p. 58). Once you notice poor posture, in yourself and others, it's all that you can see. "I see poor posture . . ."

The first reason that I'm including this tip is as a general plea for those of us who sit at desks to become more aware of our posture. It's beyond the scope of this book to detail the many dangers of poor posture and a sedentary lifestyle, but since I'm encouraging you to do work that could keep many of you more attached to your chairs, I must perform my due diligence by encouraging you to explore healthy posture resources and adjust accordingly.

Aside from my concern for your health, the second reason for this tip is that I've learned that great posture plays well on camera. It demonstrates clear, assertive, and engaging presence. Without going down the rabbit hole around power postures, I will say that in my work as a yoga teacher and teacher in higher education, I have found that how I carry myself impacts how I communicate. On the flip side, as an audience member or student, how teachers carry themselves influences my learning experience.

It's easy to explore this idea for yourself. Sit down and hunch over. Collapse your spine and belly. Then, still in this slumped posture, introduce yourself to a pretend audience. Notice how that feels. Now, sit up straight. If you're sitting on a chair with a back, don't use the back of the chair. Imagine that a string is attached to the top of your head and it's being pulled toward the ceiling. Introduce yourself again. Did you notice a difference?

When recording your videos, practice perfect posture to convey your most confident self to your students. Who knows? Maybe taking time to demonstrate great posture while recording your videos will ripple off into other areas of your life, helping you develop a new posture habit that will carry you forward, head held high.

References

Edwards, M. (2016, May 30). *YogAlign: Change your posture, change your life.* Workshop presented at Kripalu Yoga Centre, Stockbridge, MA.

Shyamalan, M.K. (1999). *The Sixth Sense.* Retrieved from http://www .lexwilliford.com/Workshops/Screenwriting/Scripts/Adobe%20Acrobat%20 Scripts/Sixth%20Sense.pdf

TIP 62: THE CAMERA WILL EAT YOUR ENERGY

◀◀ ∣ ▶▶

As I mentioned in the introduction, my high school media class used to produce a morning news show. I'll never forget one morning when I was the anchor of the show, which is to say that I read the announcements about sports scores and after-school clubs. Hard-hitting news, folks.

I'd been doing the show for a few weeks, but that morning I was feeling a little more confident and a lot cheekier, so I decided to be a bit over the top. I was nodding my head and raising my eyebrows, just like the anchors that you see on television, and really hamming it up. I thought I was just acting a little goofy in the name of fun, but after the show, for the rest of the day, students and teachers complimented me.

"You were so good," they said. "You looked like a real news anchor."

That was a light bulb moment for me. I realized then that the camera eats our energy. If you speak in your normal tone of voice with your usual mannerisms, it will fall flat onscreen. If you are exceptionally animated, more so than you might be in person, you will come off as just right on camera, because the camera will eat some of that extra energy.

I presented about video presentation skills at a conference a few years ago. An attendee who worked with online faculty at his institution came up to me afterward and told me that if there was one thing he wished his faculty knew, it was that the camera was eating their energy. He told me he was continually reminding folks to be a bit peppier in their videos, but he hadn't had the language to explain it. I encouraged him to feel free to borrow my energy-eating lingo.

Add a little punch to your instructional videos. Enunciate. Use your hands. Move your head and make facial expressions. Go high energy. Think of your favorite broadcaster and mimic them. For some of us, this will feel uncomfortable at first, but I promise you that when you watch the video back, the camera will have eaten some of that energy, bringing you down to a reasonable level of "oomph." Experiment with this, finding your ideal oomph-level. If it helps, try creating a video like this and tell yourself that as soon as you watch it back, you're going to delete it. It will never see the light of day. Permit yourself to step outside your comfort zone, knowing that to start, it's just between you and your camera.

Too many instructional videos show a very well-intentioned individual who looks like a deer in the headlights. Smile! Laugh! Move! Your videos will be better for it.

Position your smartphone's camera over Figure 62.1 to view a video about this tip.

Figure 62.1. Video: *The Camera Eats Your Energy.*

Note. Retrieved from https://youtu.be/nVIIHt6QXwA

TIP 63: KEEP IT GENERAL

◄◄ ❙ ►►

Of all the tips that I'm sharing with you in this book, this is the tip that I most wish I had known about when I first started creating videos. I'm so excited to share it with all of you, because I know that it would've made my life much easier in those early days of creating videos, and I'm confident that as you start your video creation journey, you will find this tip very useful. As always, if this tip doesn't vibe with you and your teaching, just set it aside and focus on what works.

Let me start by explaining to you how I used to make videos. I would include tons of details in my videos, like comments on the current weather in my area, mentions of holidays ("Happy Valentine's Day, everyone!") and specific due dates for course assignments ("Now that we've reviewed the upcoming project, remember to submit it by Tuesday, March 24th at 11:59 p.m.").

I thought that being very specific in my videos was the best thing for student learning. It might have been, but guess what? It was terrible for me as a teacher. As soon as I added those kinds of details to a video, I was stamping a big ticking time bomb on it. I could never use those videos again. Term after term, I would create and recreate videos. It took me several semesters of doing this before the light bulb went off in my head. I started to wonder if I could limit details and dates and still produce videos that were beneficial to my students.

I gave it a try. I created a term's worth of videos with no specifics. I didn't mention the holidays or the weather. I didn't ask if my students' favorite team had won the Super Bowl or World Series. Most importantly, I never mentioned due dates in my videos. Instead, I would say something along the lines of, "Make sure to check the course announcements page for this week's deadlines."

The result was nothing short of transformational for my teaching and life. I gained back a ton of time that I would've otherwise spent on recreating videos each term. My students were still getting the same high-quality information as always. I used those videos for quite a while. That said, I've found that after about a year, I do feel the urge to redo my videos in order to share new ideas and refresh the content. But I make that decision on my terms.

Keep in mind that if you change your course's assignments (or instructional designers change assignments for a course that you teach), you will likely need to update your videos. Such is life. It's not realistic to assume that you can make a batch of videos once and never need to update them. However, by avoiding specific details and dates in your videos, you'll create a much more sustainable video creation process.

TIP 64: BREVITY IS THE ORDER OF THE DAY

◄◄ ▌ ►►

One of my favorite books, *Brain Rules* by John Medina (2008), considers the ideal amount of time for a lecture: 10 minutes. If you go past 10 minutes, you are likely to lose your students' attention. Here's a fundamental rule of brain science: For information to transfer through students' sensory and memory systems, ideally ending up in their long-term memory where they can apply the concepts in a variety of situations, you need to have students' attention first. If there's no attention, there's no learning.

Some of you might be thinking, "Well, it's not my problem if my students choose not to pay attention. It's my job to give them this information. It's their job to learn it." I must disagree. Our job is to teach. In the twenty-first century, we know enough about how the brain works and how students learn best to make small, simple, and powerful teaching choices. One of those choices can be to be mindful of attention and cognitive load.

If you have 30 minutes of content that you want to cover in a video lecture, I suggest the following: First, if you believe that lecture is indeed the best way to convey that information, break that content into 3 lectures of 10 minutes each. Provide a summary of each video so students know what content will be covered in each. Second, ask yourself if a lecture is the best way to teach that information. Could students participate in an interactive discussion instead? Do an online scavenger hunt? Could you require students to perform research on the content and present their findings to the class? What about having students blog about their reaction to an infographic? I could go on and on here, but the point is that while lecture is a part of my teaching toolbox, it's just a single tool; I use many others, selecting the best tool for the job.

My ideal length of time for a video is about 5 minutes. Now, in truth, when I get talking to my students in my videos and I'm feeling pumped about the work that we're doing together, that 5 minutes goes by in a flash. My videos usually come in around 7 or 8 minutes. I could probably cut down on time by creating a detailed outline of what I want to talk about and sticking to that outline, but you know what? That doesn't sound like very much fun to me, which means that it won't be a sustainable practice. I keep making videos because they are so much fun, and as long as I'm aware of my time and keep it less than 10 minutes, I'm happy.

As you record your first couple of videos, take a second to jot down how long you think it will take and how long it actually takes. If you are consistently going over 10 minutes, it's worth considering other options. If you're remaining under 10 minutes, you're probably in good shape. If you can stay at 5 minutes in each video, you have much more self-control than I do, so congrats!

Reference

Medina, J. (2008). *Brain rules: 12 principles for surviving and thriving at work, home, and school.* Seattle, WA: Pear Press.

TIP 65: ALLOW EXTRA TIME AT FIRST

◄◄ | ►►

In today's world, time is our most precious resource. It's important to schedule your video recording into your day. To do that, let's explore how much time it will take you to record and share your videos with your students.

Consider 3 buckets of time as a beginner: preparation, recording, and uploading/sharing. Preparing to record your video will consist of deciding what type of video you'll create and what you'll say or do in that video. This will vary by person, but let's allow for 10 to 15 minutes. As a beginner, even though I've encouraged you to make mistakes and keep going, your mistakes might be super-sized when you first start off. If you drop a string of curses after stumbling over your words, for example, you don't want to keep that take. To start, estimate that you'll want to record 3 takes before you find your final version. In this example, that's 15 minutes. Finally, you'll want to upload and share your video. Assuming that you have high-speed Internet, it shouldn't take too long to upload the video—a few minutes should suffice. Sharing is as simple as copying and pasting the link and adding a few lines of text to explain the video, so we'll allow 5 minutes there.

In total, for a beginner, you'll want to allow between 30 and 40 minutes to create your first video. By budgeting for that, you will prevent yourself from rushing or getting overwhelmed. Run through your first video and notice how long each step takes you. Typically, with each subsequent recording, you'll see that the time it takes you to create a video gets shorter. I can record and share a 5-minute video in less than 10 minutes, and while the video is uploading, I'm working on something else so that I don't lose that time.

Allow for some extra time at first, but know that you'll eventually become very efficient as a video producer and your videos will start to pay you back in the time that they save you by boosting student learning and reducing redundant questions.

TIP 66: EXPLAIN THE VIDEO'S RELEVANCE

◀◀ I ▶▶

Relevance is a foundational element of great teaching and learning. If something is relevant to me, I can see how it relates to my life. If, for example, I attended a conference with two workshop offerings in the 9:00 a.m. time slot, one about calculus and the other about online teaching strategies, I would choose the latter because it is most relevant for me. Sometimes, relevance is crystal clear. Other times we, as teachers, need to help our students see how concepts relate to their lives.

Relevance is a key factor in the theory of andragogy, made popular by Malcolm Knowles beginning in the 1950s (Aubrey & Riley, 2016). In general, proponents of andragogy agree that for adult learners, relevance is an integral part of the learning experience. Adult learners need to understand how a course concept will relate to their lives. How will they use that concept at home, at school, at work, or in their communities? Understanding those connections will increase their achievement and satisfaction.

Make ample use of relevance in your videos. A great phrase that you can use to explain relevance is "This video will help you to . . ." and then fill in the rest. You could also say, "By watching this video, you will . . ." and then articulate some possible ways that the video's content will help students or apply to their lives.

A note to keep in mind is that students' future career prospects do not need to be the sole basis for conversations about relevance. I think that's a big misconception. We can also help students see relevance by realizing that course content will help them to become a better thinker, writer, or human being. Relevance can apply to not only students' careers but also their role as a college student or their personal lives. For example, if I'm talking about time management in a video, I will often remind students that learning to manage their time is a skill that they can apply in my course, other courses, their entire college career, their personal lives, and their future in the workforce.

As you prepare and present a video, ask yourself how it will be relevant to your students today, tomorrow, and in the future. How can you weave that into your videos, no matter your approach or theme?

Reference

Aubrey, K., & Riley, A. (2016). *Understanding and using educational theories.* Los Angeles, CA: SAGE.

TIP 67: BREAK SOME EGGS

◀◀ | ▶▶

There's an old saying that if you want to make an omelet, you have to break some eggs. That seems to me to be a modern, Westernized version of the Eastern philosophy, "No mud, no lotus." In short, beautiful things come out of seemingly icky things. I've found this to be very true of videos and teaching in general.

My first year of teaching was a blur of creativity, excitement, and experimentation. In my second year of teaching, I started to actually get organized and be more intentional about what I was doing. A lot of the classes that I planned went well. Some didn't. Some of those "perfectly" planned classes felt like pulling teeth, and I'm not sure if I was the dentist or the patient.

I started to observe that sometimes the classes that I didn't plan seemed to have the opposite effect. I was working full-time at my institution while also teaching during my workday. Some days, the advising office where I worked would get slammed, and my planning time would disappear. I would frantically try to pull together a lesson at the last minute and run up to the classroom to teach.

Many of those poorly planned classes were some of the best that I taught, with students incredibly engaged and with high energy levels in the room. I wonder if letting go of the reins a bit and surrendering to the process of teaching and learning led to that positive energy. I imagine that was a big part of it.

When you make your videos, notice if you're holding on too tight. One way to see this is if you feel like you have to start over with every mistake. You don't. Name the mistake, or don't, but keep going. Let the video and your teaching be natural, human, and flawed. The energy in that type of video will be 10 times more engaging than if you try to perform to someone else's idea of what a video should look like.

It's okay to break some eggs in your video. It's okay to flub your words or to veer a bit off track. I'd rather appear human and flawed than robotic and stiff. I've been using this style of video for over 10 years, and the feedback that I've received from my students tells me that they don't mind my mistakes; in fact, I think they welcome them.

Go ahead and break some eggs. Roll around in the mud. Let go of the reins and see where your videos will take you and your students. Omelets and lotus flowers await you.

SECTION EIGHT

USING POWERPOINT IN YOUR VIDEOS

Do you believe that coincidences have a greater meaning? I do. I prefer the term *synchronicity* and believe in a meaning behind everything. For example, just as I started to write this section, while taking a well-deserved writing break, I hopped on Twitter, where tweets from an education conference bombarded me, many of which included pictures of people's slide presentations. All of the slides that I saw were covered in text. What perfect synchronicity.

PowerPoint has become practically ubiquitous in higher education (and the conferences that support it), yet many of us are ignoring principles of design and presentation in our PowerPoint slides. If a doctor or lawyer makes bad slides, so be it. Who can blame them? It's not their field of expertise. We, however, are educators. We need to step up our PowerPoint game.

The tips in this section will help those of you who choose to use PowerPoints in your videos to do so effectively, applying principles of brain-based teaching and cognitive load to your design and presentation choices. Hopefully, what you gain from this chapter will ripple out into the rest of your work, spread to your colleagues, and start a PowerPoint revolution in higher education. We need one. It's time to reclaim this useful tool and to end the tyranny of boring, poorly designed PowerPoint presentations. The time is now, and the job is ours. If not us, who? If not now, when?

TIP 68: TELLING
ISN'T TEACHING

◄◄ I ►►

If telling were teaching, we'd all be so smart we could hardly stand it.

—Robert Mager, *Developing Attitude Toward Learning,* 1968

One of my core beliefs about teaching is that all teachers should spend time reflecting on and defining what the words *teaching* and *telling* mean to them. For a long time in our country's educational history, the terms were synonymous. In our modern era, however, and with the hard work of many classroom teachers and educational theorists, most people now realize that telling is not the same as teaching. Teaching has evolved into a relationship between students and teachers, where there is a mutual construction of knowledge. All of our research on great teaching points to the importance of active learning, where students become active participants in the learning experience rather than passive recipients.

The use of PowerPoint in our classrooms and videos seems to be a focal point for this shift. PowerPoint is a tremendous tool that has, in many ways, revolutionized teaching and learning. It is also widely misused, and in my observations, that misuse is due in large part to a shift back toward telling over teaching, or passive over active learning.

Have you ever sat in a class or workshop that consisted of the teacher or presenter reading a series of slides to you, word-for-word off the slides? I have. Did you wonder to yourself, *Why is he reading this to me? I know how to read.* Did this approach capture your attention and inspire you to learn more? If offered the choice, would you have opted to take another class or workshop with that teacher?

Reading PowerPoints is telling, not teaching. It is the quintessential example of a so-called teaching choice that sets up a passive learning experience. I would argue that the phrase *passive learning* is an oxymoron. Unless we are actively engaged with the new information available to us, we will not learn and retain that information for very long. I might be able to recall a phone number that someone reads to me for the time it takes to dial it, but that's not learning. As soon as I dial that number, that information leaves my brain, filtered out by a very effective brain system that doesn't retain worthless details. Active learning requires work, engagement, and activity on the part of the learner. Those elements are what moves information from our senses into our long-term memory stores, where we can then apply it in a variety of situations.

If you choose to create video lectures using PowerPoint, or any types of presentation slides or documents, remember that telling isn't teaching. Reading your slides to your students will bore you and them. If you're creating this type of video, make sure to use strategies like providing examples, building on students' prior knowledge, asking questions, pausing to give students a chance for self-reflection, or telling stories to keep your students engaged.

Reference

Mager, R. F. (1968). *Developing attitude toward learning*. Palo Alto, CA: Fearon Publishers.

TIP 69: APPLY BASIC DESIGN PRINCIPLES

◀◀ I ▶▶

Following are three very simple design principles that you can utilize to create engaging PowerPoint slides (Reynolds, 2012) that will support your video lectures:

1. Use images.
2. Limit text.
3. Use one idea per slide.

Before we go deeper, let me warn you: These rules will ruin you as an audience member or a student. Once you learn these design principles and begin to master them, you'll start to notice that most people aren't using them. It can make it feel impossible to sit through a poorly designed presentation. That said, knowledge is power. I would rather come out from under the veil of PowerPoint denial and make great slide decks for myself and my students than continue to live in obliviousness.

First, make ample use of images, typically one compelling image per slide. Let that image represent the key point of the slide. PowerPoint is now easily integrated with access to open content that is free for all users, so you should have no problem finding images that will catch your audience's attention. You don't need an image on every slide—my favorite slide type is a short quote written in black text on a clean, white slide. However, at least some images should be woven throughout your presentation. Of course, make sure to include alt text for your images, and if presenting in person or via video, your speech should provide a brief description of your image in support of accessibility for all learners.

Second, limit the amount of text contained on each slide. Your slides are not your speaker notes (see tip 70). Your slides are meant to capture your students' attention. I've seen some recommendations state that the ideal limit is 5 words per slide. I've tried that route, and it's very difficult. That said, I'm very intentional about the text that makes it onto my slides, and I drastically limit the amount of text I use. I think 10 words is a more reasonable limit.

Third, you should only cover one idea per slide. That might mean that you end up with more slides than you are used to from previous presentations. This is a good sign of your progress. Most of us know that in writing, we want to focus on only one main idea per paragraph. The same is true of PowerPoint slides. By focusing on one idea per slide, you'll help your students focus.

Like anything else in life, it might take some time to master these three design principles. Start where you are and set an intention to follow them. Even starting to limit your text a bit and use more images is a step in the right direction. What is most important, I feel, to integrating these tools into your teaching is to start noticing how it feels to be a student or audience member receiving a poorly designed presentation. Those experiences were what motivated me to make some changes in my teaching, and I've come to appreciate what a difference it can make to my engagement when a presenter uses a few basic principles of design.

Reference

Reynolds, G. (2012). *Presentation Zen: Simple ideas on presentation design and delivery*. Berkeley, CA: New Riders.

TIP 70: USE YOUR SLIDES TO PRESENT IDEAS, NOT AS SPEAKER NOTES

◀◀ ❙ ▶▶

Repeat after me: "My PowerPoint slides are not my speaker notes." This is a critical point for those of you who are planning to use PowerPoint in your videos. Increasingly, I've been noticing people using slides that include all their content, with line after line of text. I've realized that many people rely on their slides as speaker notes. Slides are not speaker notes. They are meant to grab the audience's attention and to illustrate (which means to visually display) critical content. Then, you, as the speaker, add in additional information in spoken form.

If you plan to present a PowerPoint in person, you can often use the notes feature in PowerPoint and hide the notes from your audience by using presentation mode. This means that the audience will only see the slides projected, but you'll also have access to your notes on your computer. However, if you're recording a screencast of a PowerPoint presentation, presentation mode won't work because your screencast recording software is going to capture exactly what is on your screen, notes included. You have a couple of options here if you're creating videos that require some speaker notes.

You might be tempted to revert to the old method of just using your slides as your speaker notes. This can sometimes feel like the easiest and least time-consuming course of action. *What's the big deal?* you might think. The big deal is that the fastest way to lose someone's attention is to put a text-heavy PowerPoint slide in front of them. It goes against everything we know about how the brain learns best. Resist that urge. There's a better option.

When creating your slide deck, use best principles of design to create great slides that will engage your students. Enter as many notes as you need in the speaker notes section. Then, you can easily print those notes to have handy when you are recording your video lecture. To print your notes, go to "Print" and then select "Outline." This will print an outline of your slides with your speaker notes included.

Then, when you present and record your lecture, run a Slideshow presentation so that only your slides appear on screen. You can choose whether to add your headshot video. Have your notes handy. Just as you would in any other lecture or presentation, feel free to glance down at your notes throughout your presentation, making sure to return your eye contact to the camera (tip 60) regularly. It's okay to glance at your notes as needed, as long as you return to making eye contact with the camera. Your students don't expect you to have a teleprompter handy. You could even hold the notes up as a prop and use them to emphasize key points. Remember: We're highlighting our humanity and expertise in our videos, not our perfectionism.

Another simple option, going old school, is to write your notes on flashcards. I still do this for many of my presentations. I use one note card per slide, which helps me to stay organized. I never try to force my speaker notes into my slides, though. Those are meant for my audience, not for me.

I think that sometimes teachers feel like they have to keep constant eye contact in a video lecture, so they make a choice to put all their content on their slides rather than using typed or written notes. And the road to hell is paved with good intentions, right? A video will be much more compelling if you use good slide design and need to occasionally look at your notes than if you are reading tons of text off a slide.

Since PowerPoint is so widely used, getting clear about how to use our slides and how our slides differ from speaker notes seems to be a shift that can have a big impact on teaching and learning. When you record videos, make sure to use your slides and speaker's notes appropriately.

Position your smartphone's camera over Figure 70.1 to view a video about this tip.

Figure 70.1. Video: *Use Your Slides to Present Ideas.*

Note. Retrieved from https://youtu.be/QghMmItNqlk

TIP 71: UNDERSTAND THE NEUROSCIENCE OF POWERPOINT

◀◀ I ▶▶

One of my fields of study is brain-based teaching (BBT). Sometimes also called neuroeducation, it considers how principles of neuroscience influence teaching and learning. A fundamental tenet of BBT is that the brain is the primary organ of learning, so helping teachers to better understand how the brain works will improve their teaching. This has certainly been true for me.

Although many facets of BBT are beyond the scope of this book, I see such a significant reliance on PowerPoint that I want to devote a tip to helping you understand some key neuroscientific principles that influence how students receive information presented to them via PowerPoint. I think many of you will likely incorporate this tip. This will help you make more informed decisions about how to create and present videos that include PowerPoint.

Jared Cooney Horvath's (2014) article from *Mind, Brain, and Education,* "The Neuroscience of PowerPoint," explains this research in detail. The key takeaway is that if students are reading your slides, they aren't listening to you. "This suggests that silent reading (the kind most often done by audience members attempting to decipher text presented on a [PowerPoint] slide) utilizes the same perceptual networks as the aural speech listening" (Horvath, 2014, pp. 137–138). In short, if you are putting a large amount of text on your slides, that text is competing with your speech for students' attention.

Horvath (2014) found that "dividing attention between text and speech typically impairs comprehension and retention for both stimuli streams" (p. 139). If you use too much text in your presentations, students won't remember much of that text or much of what you are saying to them. Horvath goes on to recommend limiting text on slides and utilizing more image-based presentations (images utilize a different processing path in the brain). Another strategy that I sometimes employ when I use text on my slides is to pause and ask students to read that text quietly to themselves. Then, I'll begin to speak about it in more detail.

The brain will not effectively process text-heavy presentations combined with your verbal content. Be mindful of this principle when creating your videos. If you're going to record screencasts with slides, limit your text on slides, use more images, and pause as needed to give students (and their brains) time to read the content.

Reference

Horvath, J. C. (2014). The neuroscience of PowerPoint. *Mind, Brain, and Education, 8*(3), 137–142.

TIP 72: COMPLEMENT YOUR POWERPOINT-BASED LECTURES WITH STRUCTURED NOTES

◄◄ I ►►

I am a huge fan, both as a student and a teacher, of structured notes. While the intricacies of note-taking systems are beyond the scope of this book, I want to give you a couple of ideas to help your students get the most out of your video lectures. I think of structured notes as helping students get more bang for their buck. Many of us struggle to maintain attention in today's busy world, and I've found that structured notes are a way to harness focus and improve concentration.

Structured notes complement video lectures. One straightforward method is to download a PDF file of your PowerPoint presentation in handout form. If you select the option for "Handouts" with three slides per page, you'll have handouts with several lines printed next to each slide. Post these handouts in your learning management system along with your video, and encourage students to print them and use them for note-taking. Of course, not all of our students have easy access to printers, so I want to give you and your students some additional options.

In tip 19, you learned about using graphic organizers (also known as concept maps) to present ideas. You can also encourage students to use this method when taking notes on your video lectures. Students can draw a circle at the center of a piece of paper and continue to add layers of ideas in additional circles. This is an excellent option for students who enjoy drawing, and no printing is required. I've had students take this to the next level and color-code their graphic organizers.

My final suggestion is to introduce students to the Cornell Note-Taking Method, which is a very simple method of organizing one's notes. If you Google this method with the word *template*, you'll find access to a ton of note-taking templates that you can share with your students. Students can print and take handwritten notes (my preference). Another option is for students to open a Cornell template in Word and type their notes into the document. This will work for your students who don't have a printer. They could set up their screen so that your lecture is on one side and the template is on the other, or they could view your video on their phone while taking notes on their computer.

Many of our students have never been taught how to take and use effective notes. Including this method with your videos will help your students to become active learners. Don't forget to encourage students to make use of those notes regularly in consistent study sessions. Taking notes is only half of the equation; using them for study and recall is the other half.

SECTION NINE

IS BEING ON CAMERA FOR EVERYONE?

L et me cut to the chase and answer the question in the title of this section. No! While most of you reading this book will enjoy being on camera or at least make peace with it, some of you will discover that you're just too uncomfortable for on-camera videos. That discomfort will translate into disengagement with your students. This is okay. I don't know of anything that's for everyone. Chocolate, maybe?

While some of you will opt to avoid on-camera videos, others might be wavering. You're nervous about it, but you might also recall prior experiences where you worked through your fears and found something great on the other side. You're hesitant but open to the experience.

If you're ready for your close-up and can't wait to be on camera, you can probably skip this section. Although if you think you might want to mentor other faculty in developing videos in the future, I encourage you to read it. It might not apply to you but could support you in helping others down the road.

If you're either hesitant about being on camera, or confident that it's not for you, this chapter will help you explore that decision. This is a no-shame section, so know that whatever you decide, your choices will be supported, and I'll offer you some effective alternatives. Just because you're not going to be on camera today, doesn't mean you won't be in the future. You can still make videos for yourself and your students while honoring your unique needs and strengths.

TIP 73: TAKE THE WOOL SWEATER TEST

◄◄ ❙ ►►

As a young girl, I was a competitive swimmer. Six days a week, I'd spend a couple of hours at swim practice. Afterward, we'd all rinse the chlorine out of our hair and throw on our clothes. I distinctly remember how awful that could be during the winter, putting an itchy wool sweater onto my still-wet skin and feeling the moisture from my hair drip down the back of my neck. To this day, you won't catch me in a wool sweater. In my mind, it is the epitome of discomfort. For some people, this is what it feels like when a camera starts recording them.

After many years of making videos and teaching faculty how to create their own videos, here is my unofficial statistical analysis of how people feel about being on camera: 20% of people enjoy it and are "all in." Another 60% of people are initially hesitant, but with time and practice, they grow to appreciate the benefits and feel comfortable. Finally, the remaining 20% of people are just not comfortable being on camera and are better suited to creating other types of videos such as screencasts.

Only you can determine in which bucket you belong. The trick is, initial hesitance does not mean you will never feel comfortable. Everything in life takes practice. I encourage you to give headshot-style videos a try at least a couple of times before you make your decision.

That said, if being on camera feels like putting on a wool sweater after swim practice, as if you've never been so uncomfortable in your entire life, then trust yourself and that feeling. Headshot videos are not the only type of video that you can create. There are plenty of other options for you to consider.

TIP 74: PRACTICE MAKES PERFECT

◀◀ I ▶▶

You've probably heard the adage that practice makes perfect, but do you know the science behind it? When we learn a new skill, neurons in our brains form a neural pathway associated with that skill. When we practice deliberately, a substance called myelin (a fatty acid) coats that neural pathway, making the connections stronger and faster (somewhat akin to high-speed Internet in our brains) (Coyle, 2009).

Remember the first time that you tried to ride a bike? "What is this awkward machine that you are forcing me to sit on, Mom?! Don't you love me? Ahhhhh . . . <crash>." If we judged our skill at bike riding by our first bike ride, there would be no bikes.

I've learned a lot about the power of practice since becoming a mother myself. I watched my young son go from tapping out random sounds on the keyboard to playing songs at his first piano recital, thanks to regular practice. I've seen him go from sounding out Dr. Seuss books to happily reading feature articles in *Sports Illustrated*. How did he get from step A to step B? Practice. With each practice session, myelin coated his neural pathways and strengthened that skill.

One of my greatest desires in life is to be perfect at a new skill the first time that I try it. Wouldn't that be nice? Sadly, our brains don't work like that. Behind every talented individual is a lifetime of practice.

You might be nervous about creating videos in general, or about being on camera specifically. Your first videos might feel like falling off your bike. Your videos won't be perfect to begin, and in truth, I'm not sure that perfection is even my goal for my videos. I want to continue to enjoy the creative process, to help my students, and to connect with them on a human level. Let's focus, then, on practice and progress, not perfection.

Can you be willing to give your video creation process time to evolve? Can you let go of your ideas of a perfect video and instead focus on regular practice? Don't assume that every video will feel like the first few. Just like you can now probably enjoy the gift of a bike ride without crashing in front of the entire neighborhood, so too, with some practice, you will likely come to enjoy the creative gift of making educational videos.

For those of you deciding about being on camera, take this science to heart. Your hesitation or discomfort are very likely temporary conditions that can be cured with practice.

Reference

Coyle, D. (2009). *The talent code: Greatness isn't born. It's grown. Here's how.* New York, NY: Bantam.

TIP 75: ARE YOU A DEER IN THE HEADLIGHTS?

◀◀ I ▶▶

In this section, we're exploring together how to decide which types of videos are the best fit for you. Headshot videos where you are on camera are not ideal for every person. A factor that I invite you to consider when making this decision is your on-camera presence. Few of us will be video superstars on camera, but most of us will be able to create an engaging, high-energy video that captures our students' attention. Finally, and I say this with love, there might be a handful of folks who, despite their best efforts, create what I call "deer in the headlights"–type videos.

Headshot videos are a fantastic way to engage with students in both online and flipped classrooms. However, I don't think that a bad video is better than none at all. A bad video can be disengaging and just plain dull.

Follow the system outlined in this book. Try the practice exercises in Section Twelve. If, after you follow those steps, you watch your videos back and notice that your energy, despite your best efforts, is very flat and that your videos are disengaging, consider alternate options like screencasts. Trust yourself, but you might also want to send your videos to a trusted friend (the good type of friend who will be honest with you in the kindest way possible). Ask your friend if your video is engaging and interesting and whether you have a strong on-camera presence. If not, you might find that the camera is just a bit too scary for you and that you can add much more energy to a screencast with an audio recording. Perhaps the camera freezes you, just like a deer in the headlights, and by removing it from the equation, you'll find your best screen presence by being off-screen.

After creating several videos, evaluate your on-screen presence. Are you frozen and mechanical? Is your affect (tone of voice) flat or dynamic? Would you and your students be better served by a different type of video such as a screencast with audio only?

Of course, if you make the decision to focus on screencasts to begin, know that this can change. After getting comfortable with screencasts, circle back and try some on-camera videos. You might just find that your on-camera presence has evolved.

TIP 76: TRY SCREENCASTS WITH AUDIO ONLY

◀◀ I ▶▶

You learned about screencasts in tip 40. I want to take some time in this tip to speak specifically to those of you who have discovered that being on camera is not your thing. Either you feel uncomfortable, or you've recognized that your on-camera presence falls flat, but you still want to find an engaging alternative for your students.

You can create tremendously engaging, interesting, fun, and creative videos without being on camera. I don't want any of you to think that screencasts with audio only are second-best; that's just not true. While I'm a huge fan of the benefits of headshot-style videos, that doesn't mean they are the only way to create an awesome instructional video. If you pour your energy and passion into your screencasts, even if they only contain audio, you can still transform your teaching.

I have watched many high-energy, loud, vivacious individuals go completely flat when a camera turns on. Solution? Don't use the camera. Record a screencast with audio instead. Not being on camera removes some energy-eating pressure. That said, it's important to channel your energy into your voice. Hopefully, taking away the pressure of a camera will help you to add some panache to the audio that accompanies your screencasts.

Also, remember that just because you aren't on camera doesn't mean you should abandon the humanizing elements of videos. When we are only using screencasts, there can be a temptation to get hyperfocused on logistical or lecture-type videos. Make sure you are weaving some personal touches such as stories into your videos. You could also create a simple "About Me" PowerPoint slide with pictures and introduce yourself to your students by screencasting the slide along with your audio introduction.

Be creative, and remember that you can still be human, real, and engaging without being on camera.

TIP 77: GET ANIMATED

◄◄ I ►►

If you've decided to forgo being on camera, you can use screencasts with audio only, but another option is to create an animated video starring your very own avatar. This probably sounds like something that would be hugely time-consuming and have a big learning curve, right? It's not. We live in an era with many edtech tools that support excellent teaching. Some of them even meet our criteria of being simple and sustainable.

I'm always a little hesitant to recommend a tool in print, knowing that solutions come and go, but this is a resource that I've been using for many years, so I'm confident it will remain with us for years to come. For animated videos, Powtoon (www.powtoon.com) is your next best friend. Let me be clear that as with most of these types of technologies, there's both a paid and free version. For our simple videos, the free version is sufficient.

Powtoon includes tons of predesigned templates that allow you to create animated videos for your students. Simply plug in your own text and content, save, and share. I've created Powtoons for students to introduce assignments in a unique and fun way. As an online student, I've used Powtoons for my final projects. It's a nice change of pace from PowerPoint.

While the templates are the easiest solution, you can absolutely customize several elements of your video, including your avatar. Again, Powtoon is very intuitive, so you should be able to teach yourself the basics by just clicking around and exploring. Remember, our goal is not to create the world's best Powtoon of all time but, rather, to create a simple video that will help us connect with our students.

I know that many teachers who prefer staying off camera love Powtoon, sometimes even deciding to invest in the paid version, because they can be very creative with it, infusing their personality into their animations, while remaining behind the camera. If creativity is a priority for you, but you feel that being on camera is the right choice for you, check out Powtoon to create an awesome instructional video.

Position your smartphone's camera over Figure 77.1 to view a video about this tip.

Figure 77.1. Video: *Get Animated.*

Note. Retrieved from https://youtu.be/XIow3dhGKfsAU

TIP 78: A SPECIAL NOTE FOR INDIVIDUALS FROM DIVERSE BACKGROUNDS

Safety, Security, and Social Change

◀◀ I ▶▶

Recently, a friend of mine shared on social media that he'd been talking to a group of faculty about creating videos for their students. One woman shared with him that she felt too exposed in videos and felt unsafe revealing herself that way in her online courses, particularly in front of her male students. Before I discuss this anecdote further, let me emphasize that I paraphrased her concerns, and I hope that I did them justice.

This was an "aha moment" for me. I've worked with tons of faculty who are hesitant to be on camera. No one has ever articulated this particular concern to me. I'm embarrassed to say that I wasn't more intentional about inquiring about this possibility. While I identify as an intersectional feminist, which was thankfully part of my undergraduate sociology training, I carry significant privilege in this world, and I imagine that this privilege, at least in part, fed my ignorance about this topic.

I also have to consider that I've been training in video production since my junior year of high school. For me, strange as it might sound to some of you, I sometimes feel safer in my videos than I do elsewhere. Videos empower me. I didn't realize that for some, the opposite is true.

The responses to my friend's comments about this issue on social media were enlightening and frustrating. Many people responded with suggestions for alternative types of videos. *Yes*, that's a great idea, and *no* it's not okay that women feel scared to use this educational tool in support of their success and the success of their students. I also think it's highly probable that other individuals from diverse backgrounds could potentially feel unsafe when appearing on camera in videos.

I wanted to take a moment in this book to open up this conversation as a starting point. Critically, I hope that it's obvious that we need to do much more as a society to help women, people of color, trans folx, people with disabilities, and other diverse individuals feel safe. In the meantime, as it relates to videos, I have a couple of thoughts to address this challenge more specifically.

Of course, if you don't feel safe being on camera, please do consider one of the alternatives mentioned in this chapter. If you decide to create on-camera videos, be intentional about what you share with your students. You can share your personality without sharing personal details. The weather is always a great topic, for example. Perhaps you feel comfortable sharing the title of your favorite book or the reason that you got into teaching. You never need to tell students the name of the city where you live or any details about your family life, unless you feel comfortable doing so.

Finally, I want to reassure you that in 13 years of making video, I've never been the recipient of any negative, threatening, or concerning behaviors from my students. I can only speak from my experience, but I have found videos to be a safe space in my teaching. That said, I hope that you have a supervisor and institutional support system that you can notify if you are the recipient of any inappropriate behavior.

This is newer territory for me, so I don't have all the answers, but I hope we can continue this conversation. I'm setting an intention to be more direct in asking people about their concerns about being on camera, and, hopefully, we can answer those challenges with additional layers of support.

SECTION TEN

SHARING VIDEOS WITH YOUR STUDENTS

The tips in this section will help you decide the most effective and efficient way to share the videos that you create with your students. A word of caution is needed here: Anyone who writes a book that includes a reference to technology is risking that this technology will vanish, will be bought out by another company and renamed, or will be *smushed* (that's an official tech term) by a better tool. It's the nature of the beast.

I trust that the tips I've included will help you understand the types of factors to consider when sharing your videos. No matter how technology changes, these tips will provide you with the information that you need to make the best decisions for you and your students. Within the simple and sustainable model, remember to always look for technologies that will meet your needs. Fancy tech tools abound, and there's always a brilliant person behind them who will try to convince you that forgoing their tool is a disservice to your role as an educator. Buyer beware.

After reading this section, you will understand the current technologies, and you'll discover my current recommendation for a simple and sustainable sharing system. In addition, this section will cover some basics around accessibility, helping you incorporate some accessible design practices into your video sharing practice to support the learning experiences of all students.

TIP 79: CONSULT FIRST

◀◀ ▌ ▶▶

It will be up to you to consider your institutional culture and decide when and who to consult about your videos. To err on the side of caution here, I'm going to advise you to consult first. Speak to your supervisor or whoever is in charge of supporting faculty with online education at your institution. Let them know you are planning to create videos and that you want to open up that conversation. Are there any guidelines for you to follow? Can they offer you any support?

In terms of sharing your videos with students, this point is particularly salient. I once worked with a teammate on my campus (a fellow early adopter) to set up a Skype advising program for our online students. We downloaded Skype onto a bunch of computers and then started a soft rollout of the service. We didn't consult with our information technology department first. They found out and shut us down because of some security concerns with Skype. It was a bummer for us, but, obviously, our great idea wasn't worth risking the safety of the entire campus network. I learned then to be a bit more cautious and to invest time in consulting with key players.

I've realized that we shouldn't consult with others just to avoid conflicts, but rather to gain the value of other points of view. This can only add nuance to our own. I recall a time when I took a class in educational policy. A former presidential candidate and state governor came to speak to our class. I'll never forget a key piece of advice that he gave us. He said that at some point, you have to have the opposing party at the table with you. You could do it proactively and work with them from the start, or you could do it reactively, after you've launched your policy or program. His advice was to get everyone at the table from the start.

Of course, the danger of that approach is that strong-minded people with their own agenda have the potential to bog down your momentum. Be mindful of this risk and clear about your goals. That said, I think the benefits of consulting are worth the risk. The potential to gain positive feedback and support is high in most institutions, I believe, as the use of video has become more mainstream. Consulting will help you make sure you're aligning with institutional policies and goals and will hopefully give you access to a support team who can help you improve your video-creation process.

One last note here is to keep the simple and sustainable process in mind. I love tech people. I really do. I also know that they will sometimes see my enthusiasm for educational technologies and throw a ton of time- and labor-intensive ideas at me that aren't simple or sustainable. As you're consulting with others, if they encourage you to create hyperproduced videos using a complex system that you won't be able to sustain, keep your mantra in mind: I am going to create simple and sustainable videos for myself and my students.

TIP 80: SHARE VIA YOUR LEARNING MANAGEMENT SYSTEM

◄◄ ❙ ►►

These days, the online learning world feels a bit like the Wild West. When I started teaching online, there were only a couple of learning management systems (LMSs), and now it seems that many more options are available to teach a course online. I share this because this tip is dynamic and ever-changing.

At this time, some LMSs allow you to record and share videos directly within their system. Others don't. Because of the aforementioned dynamism I won't say for sure that any particular LMS offers the option to record videos directly into the course, but in general, I'll say that some do, and you can investigate if your institution's current LMS offers this option. Further, there's a good chance that if you're reading this book, you might have the ability to influence decisions about whether your institution stays with your current LMS or chooses a new one. I would argue that built-in video recording options are a great selling point.

If your LMS offers the option to record video, it will likely be within course announcements, discussion responses, or in specific course content items. This is worth noting, as you might have other plans for where to place your videos (Section Five). That said, if you like the options for video placement, being able to easily record and share a video right within your LMS is tough to beat.

Consider that in most cases, you'll only be able to record headshot-type videos within your LMS. If you are planning to use screencasts, you'll probably need to choose another path. If headshot videos are your primary focus, this option will work great.

One final, and very important, point to mull over is the ability to reuse these videos. Some LMSs don't allow you to copy content from one term to the next (or at least not easily). This is a deal breaker for me. If you can easily copy videos from term to term, however, using your LMS is definitely a simple and sustainable option for sharing your videos.

TIP 81: USE YOUTUBE

◀◀ I ▶▶

YouTube has been one of my greatest tools for creating and sharing educational videos. There was a time when you could both record and share videos in YouTube. As of this printing, you can no longer record a video using YouTube. You can, however, use it to share your videos and add captions. It's simple, reasonably intuitive, and students are quite comfortable using it.

To share a video on YouTube, you'll need to create a video. You can record a video using software on your computer (e.g., QuickTime or iMovie) or by filming a video on your phone. Then, you can go either to the YouTube website or the app on your phone (make sure you have a free account created first), select the camera icon, and choose Upload Video.

However, that is not my recommended option for those of you recording on your computer. I find those video recording software programs to be confusing and time-consuming for the average user. Instead, see tip 83 for a simpler and more sustainable option for recording videos that you can then easily upload to YouTube.

No matter how you record your video, YouTube will then walk you through the uploading process, asking you to title your video and set your privacy settings. I recommend unlisted videos. Only people who have the link that you provide can access the video. I prefer this to fully public videos for the videos that I create for students.

After the video loads (this will take a few minutes), you can select Share, then copy the URL and paste this into your online classroom, an e-mail, or however you've chosen to share your videos with students. I also like to embed my videos. Embedding videos is a bit more robust than just sharing a link with students. Instead, students see a thumbnail, preview image of the video in a larger format. I use this whenever possible because it creates a nice visual that will entice students to view the video. I copy the embed link that's available within the Share menu in YouTube in addition to the URL and add that to my course announcement or discussion post. Again, to clarify, the best practice is to both embed the video and add a link to the video. When adding the link, I make sure to clearly identify it by writing "CLICK HERE to view the video" so that there's no doubt how students should proceed. Remember, many of our students are new to online learning, so we want to be very explicit in our directions to them.

If you'd like to be even more organized with your YouTube sharing, consider creating a YouTube playlist. I discuss that option in tip 84.

TIP 82: NOTE THE VIDEO'S LENGTH FOR STUDENTS

◀◀ ❙ ▶▶

Here's a very simple tip for your video creation process. In whatever space you choose to share a video with your students, make sure to note its length and a short description of the video. For example, if your video is 4 minutes and 30 seconds long, and the topic is note-taking strategies, you could create a title and heading that look something like this:

> **CLICK HERE to view video: Note-Taking Strategies (4 minutes, 30 seconds)** [This video includes an overview of the Cornell Note-Taking Method and how you can use this method to support your success in this course. You will see a Cornell template in use and be able to create your own template as a result of watching this video.]

Why do you think it's important to list the video's length? We live in a digital age where this is now a common practice. Poke around and find some videos online and you'll notice that the video's length is typically listed. Students are digital consumers who will expect this when they see a video online.

I also think that sharing this information with students demonstrates care and recognizes them as partners in the learning experience. Our students lead busy lives. A mom who is waiting to grab her son from school pickup might not have 15 minutes to watch a video, but she does have 5 minutes. If she sees the length of the video, she'll know whether she has time to watch it or if she needs to find another space in her schedule.

Listing your video's length communicates to students that we respect them and their time. It's a simple practice that will be easy to sustain. Finally, it's also a reminder to be aware of the length of our videos; we want to keep our videos to a reasonable length, because we value our own time and don't want to overload our students' cognitive load.

TIP 83: TRY THIS SIMPLE AND SUSTAINABLE RECORDING AND SHARING TOOL

◀◀ I ▶▶

It's always tough to make tech recommendations, as things seem to be in a constant state of flux, but this tool has been around for a very long time (since my first days of creating videos), so I'm confident that it will persist. My current recommendation for the most simple and sustainable way to both record and share videos is called Screencast-O-Matic (www.screencastomatic .com). I just did a little fist pump to myself as I typed that, thinking of how awesome this tool is and how many bases it covers. I hope that once you try it, you'll be just as excited.

First, as with many tech tools, there are free and paid versions. I currently use the free version, and it covers all of my video creation needs. I doubt that you'll need to opt for the paid version, but know that it's there, with all its bells and whistles, if you need it. Screencast-O-Matic takes a few minutes to download, and once you get started, you can easily select the type of video you want to record from its menu: webcam recording only (headshot type video), screencast, or webcam combined with a screencast (my favorite). Yes, they're all right there for you within one system.

The following are six simple steps to get you started. Again, this is a highly intuitive tool, so my best advice is to click around and don't be too concerned with making mistakes. You won't break anything.

1. After downloading Screencast-O-Matic, select Start Recorder. This will open the software on your computer.
2. In the Record tool, select the type of video you wish to create. If you want to record a screencast with audio only, select Screen.
3. Test your audio by speaking aloud. Remember, I recommend basic earbuds with a built-in microphone.
4. Select the small, red button labeled "Rec." You'll see a countdown begin. 3 . . . 2 . . . 1 . . . start sharing your wisdom with your students.
5. When you're done, press the red pause button (two vertical lines). If you want to delete the video, choose the trash can icon. If you want to keep and use this video, select Done.
6. You have the option to do some basic editing, but if you've kept your video simple, none will be required. Just select Save/Upload and then Upload to YouTube. Select your YouTube publish options and click Publish.

For those of you planning to add captions (see tip 85), please note that you'll need the paid version to add captions directly in Screencast-O-Matic. The paid version is very affordable (it's currently only a few dollars a month). However, you can also easily add captions directly in YouTube at no cost.

This is such a fantastic tool because it allows me to create great content for my students, and it's easy for me to use. I can't tell you how many times I've used software programs that promised me the moon, but only served to frustrate me while I tried to figure them out. I love intuitive tech tools, and Screencast-O-Matic fits the bill. In addition to my video demo (see Figure 83.1), there are ample video tutorials available on the Screencast-O-Matic website (help.screencast-o-matic.com).

Position your smartphone's camera over Figure 83.1 to view a video about this tip.

Figure 83.1. Video: *Try This Recording and Sharing Tool.*

Note. Retrieved from https://youtu.be/ZbHyo3YklAsAU

TIP 84: CREATE A YOUTUBE PLAYLIST

◀◀ ❙ ▶▶

Are you an organizer? If so, then you might love creating a YouTube playlist for your videos. A YouTube playlist is very simple; it's just a collection of your videos in a more organized format. Rather than just sharing a random bunch of videos in your YouTube channel with your students, you could create a playlist that is organized by chapter, theme, or module.

For those of you who teach multiple courses, or who plan to create multiple videos to share each week, this is an excellent option. You could have a playlist for each class that you teach as a start (e.g., ENG 100 playlist, CHEM 247 playlist). That will help you stay organized and decrease your confusion when you begin a new term.

If you plan to create more than one video per week, a playlist is a smart idea. For example, maybe you're going to create a motivational video, a video about the weekly assignments, and mini-lecture-type video each week. You can put all three of those videos into a "Week 1" playlist. Then, the following week, you can organize the next three videos into "Week 2." By grouping the videos this way, it makes it easier for both you and your students to access the content. Rather than sharing the links to individual videos, you can share the playlist link, which will encourage the students to view all related videos.

I have gone back and forth with using YouTube playlists, because I'm not the most organized person by nature, but when I do put the extra effort into creating them, I feel really good about the final product. For those of you in the specific situation of teaching multiple courses or using numerous videos, it's a solution that will help make your video creation process much more streamlined.

Want to see an example of a YouTube playlist? Use the QR code in Figure 84.1 to visit a YouTube playlist that I created for readers of this book.

Figure 84.1. YouTube Playlist: *99 Tips for Creating Simple and Sustainable Videos.*

Note. Retrieved from https://www.youtube.com/playlist?list=PLp1oNaMlolJNcLBT440n-R-4B_meQG4Ic

TIP 85: CAPTION YOUR VIDEOS

◄◄ ❙ ►►

If you haven't yet noticed, there's been a shift in higher education from a focus on accommodations to accessibility (Pryal, 2017). While this topic alone could be the subject of many books, to summarize, the accommodations model places the burden of help-seeking on the disabled student (see Pryal, 2017, for a discussion of disability language). It's up to them to ask for extra help. In the accessibility model, institutions, teachers, and presenters aim to create learning spaces and experiences that honor the needs of all types of learners.

One example of this is around captions for videos. In the former model, teachers wouldn't caption videos. If students needed captions, they would have to go through an often-arduous process to request them. In the latter model, teachers add captions without any request for accommodations. This may not only remove the burden from the disabled student but also actually benefit all students. Think about the busy parent with screaming toddlers in the background. The parent can't hear your video over the screams but can utilize your captions. My husband and I got into the habit of using captions with low sound when my son was a toddler so that we wouldn't wake him; we've kept the habit many years later and now can't watch TV without them.

Full disclosure: My captioning journey is a work in progress. I think that's true for many of us. Adding captions does add additional time to the video production process. While automatically generated captions have come a long way in recent years, they still aren't reliable. That said, it is my goal to have captions in all of my videos in the coming years.

It's also important for you to consider reaching out to the people at your institution who are experts in supporting students with disabilities to get more information on any institutional policies on accessibility in videos. There might even be support to help you add captions, so it's worth reaching out and building that relationship.

Since our ultimate goal is to create simple and sustainable videos that benefit our students and us, let's be sure not to leave any of our students behind in that process.

Position your smartphone's camera over Figure 85.1 to view a video about this tip.

Figure 85.1. Video: *Caption Your Videos*.

Note. Retrieved from https://youtu.be/1QNtmemJHIY

Reference

Pryal, K. R. G. (2017). *Life of the mind interrupted: Essays on mental health and disability in higher education.* Chapel Hill, NC: Snowraven Books.

TIP 86: DISCOVER UNIVERSAL DESIGN FOR LEARNING

◀◀ | ▶▶

In tip 85, I reviewed the importance of captioning your videos within the context of a shift from a model of disability focused on accommodations to one of accessibility. This shift is taking place in higher education, led by students and disability advocates. To review, instead of creating course content that is inaccessible for some students and then expecting those students to speak up and ask for special accommodations, we are now moving toward a model of universal accessibility.

One interesting note that I think captures this shift is that I've seen more people using captions in their Instagram videos. It seems that there is a growing awareness that inclusion is a worthy aim, not only within higher education but also as part of our broader culture. Seeing people use captions on Instagram gives me a lot of hope that new technologies will be developed that make it easier and more efficient to create video captions.

More so than in any other section of this book, this is a place where I am learning along with you. I am not an expert on accessibility, but I am an eager student. Making sure that my content is accessible to all learners is a work in progress. One of the tools that I'm using to learn more is the concept of universal design for learning (UDL). This is a model that explores how we can benefit all students by more intentional and accessible course design. The CAST organization (a nonprofit supporting UDL work) has an excellent website with a wealth of resources to get you started (udlguidelines .cast.org).

My sense of UDL is that many people discover it while trying to solve particular and practical accessibility challenges. While the focus of this book is on videos, perhaps your experience designing accessible videos will open up a new space for you in your teaching, supported by UDL. This unintentional consequence of your work with accessible videos might transform your entire outlook on teaching and course design.

SECTION ELEVEN

BUILDING YOUR VIDEO CREATION PRACTICE

In the writing world, we talk about two types of people: pantsers and planners. Pantsers write by the seat of their pants. They follow their inspiration and write in whatever direction it takes them. Planners, in contrast, approach their work with outlines, daily planners, index cards, and self-imposed deadlines.

If you are a planner, this section will feel very intuitive. If you're a total pantser, this section will help you think through your video ideas, even if you choose not to create a formal plan. In truth, I am only able to write this section out of hindsight. I started making videos in 2007 before anyone was really talking about making videos. I had to be a pantser because I didn't have a lot of guidance. You have the benefit of learning from my mistakes. While my video story turned out pretty well, I would've saved myself a lot of time and stress if I had created a plan.

You'll learn to be a bit strategic about your approach to videos, all while keeping it simple and sustainable. You'll set priorities that will allow you to make the best use of your limited time. Finally, for those of you who are feeling unsure about where to begin even after you read through these tips, don't worry. You can borrow my number one priority for videos until yours appears.

TIP 87: KEEP A
TEACHING JOURNAL

◄◄ I ►►

In tip 26, we talked about how our brains learn best and how you can use videos to capture your students' attention, a precursor for learning. Believe it or not, our brains work just like our students' brains. Where we put our attention matters. One of the ways that I harness the power of my attention is to write down important ideas, appointments, and tasks. A teaching journal is a brain-based strategy that can support your entire teaching career and your video development process in particular.

A teaching journal is different from that binder you have filled with content and activities. That's related to your curriculum and pedagogy. This teaching journal will be a tool for self-reflection and to keep track of your video plans. In this section of the book, you're going to create some goals. Write them down in your teaching journal. You can then make notes about what worked and what didn't, helping you course-correct your strategies.

Here are some things that you might want to consider in your journal:

- Include both thoughts and feelings. In higher education, we can be a bit stuck in our heads. Your feelings are valuable guides in this process. If you feel drained after creating a certain type of video, note that. If you feel ready to take on the world, that's important information too.
- Note any of your students' reactions to different types of videos. Mine their e-mails and end-of-term student evaluations for these rich data. Ask for students' opinions.
- Where are the "holes" in your course where students are still struggling? Could you use videos to improve student performance in these areas in future terms?
- What are the costs of making videos? How much time does it take you each term?
- What are the benefits of your videos? Remember, answer this question not only in terms of students but also as it pertains to you, your time, and your teaching experience.

- After completing the practice exercises in Section Twelve, note your responses in your journal.

You'll need to decide what the best modality is for your planning needs. An old-school composition book works well for this. Others might prefer to create a Google doc. I wouldn't recommend scrap paper or sticky notes; you'll want something that can stand the test of time and that you can easily return to from term to term.

By the end of one term, you should have a lot of information in your journal that you can then use to adapt your video creation process for the future.

TIP 88: DEVELOP A PLAN

◀◀ I ▶▶

The older I get, the more I realize the power of a well-laid plan. While I'm sure that there are those among you who can "wing it" and still create awesome instructional videos for your students (I know this because that's what I did in my early video days), you'll create better videos and save yourself time and frustration if you invest a bit of time in planning before you begin.

Once you decide on a system for your teaching journal, it's time to create a plan. I suggest doing some freewriting or brainstorming first. Too many of us write or ideate with our editing brains. Writing and ideating should be free flowing. You can edit later. Start by writing down everything that comes to mind when you think about creating videos. Dream big here. What types of videos come to mind? What concerns do you have? Have you seen other instructional videos that you love? What did you love about them? For which classes do you want to develop videos? When do you want to start making videos? What tools do you need? Just write. Don't second guess or worry about logistics here.

Another option is to draw a mind map. Draw the word "Video" in a circle at the center of the page and then start drawing subtopics off of that central circle. You can also use an online mind mapping software like Bubbl (www.bubbl.us). I love this method of brainstorming and find that it helps me access a more creative part of my brain than when I simply write.

In tip 89, we'll discuss how to edit and prioritize your ideas. For now, have fun with it and get it in writing. Remember that once you create a more organized and prioritized plan in the next step, you should hold onto this original brainstorming work. Some of the items that don't make it onto the prioritized list might be something that you'll want to return to in the future.

One of the great benefits to teachers in developing videos is the joy of creating. Take some time to be playful here and explore your ideas.

TIP 89: PRIORITIZE YOUR PLAN

◀◀ ❙ ▶▶

I've been teaching time management since 2006. Today, I think I'm finally starting to get the hang of it. I've realized that putting my schedule and tasks into a planner is only a small part of time management. Deciding which tasks make it into my planner (my priorities) and then setting myself up to have the motivation to complete those tasks (health and wellness) are the parts of time management that have taken me over a decade to understand.

The world will fill your schedule if you let it. I'm sure that even within your department at your institution, goals and demands are being placed on you regularly. Then, of course, there's the internal pressure to follow every good idea to wherever it wants to take you. All of this will influence your video creation journey. Setting priorities before you begin will help to increase your success and reduce frustration.

Look over the big brainstorming list that you created in tip 88. Pull out a highlighter or brightly colored marker. Circle your top three priorities from the list.

These priorities are where you begin. For some of you, your initial goals will be about preparation. You might need to create a YouTube account, for example. You might decide to purchase earbuds. Those are perfect places to start! Those who are a bit more tech-savvy might have more of the basics in place and feel ready to start recording and sharing your videos. Others of you have already played around with some videos, so you can zone in on developing content that is more intentional about supporting faculty–student relationships. You could also decide to prioritize identifying some motivational and humanizing stories to tell in your videos.

Your top three priorities should allow you to start where you are. Write them down on a new page in your teaching journal. But wait, you aren't done yet.

Beside each priority, write down the amount of time that you estimate that the goal will take for you to complete it. Then, schedule time for those tasks in your planner. Many of us miss this critical step. We live off of to-do lists that tell us what needs to be done, but then we don't create time in our schedules to do that work. Schedule this time as if it's a meeting with a very important person, because it is: you.

Finally, schedule time for "Review Video Creation Plan" in your planner. This should take place after you've completed the initial three goals. On that date, you'll pull out your teaching journal; review your progress; and, if appropriate, select your next three priorities. Again, this will vary. Some of you might feel that your work with the first three priorities is keeping you plenty busy. Others will be ready to move forward and add some new tasks to their schedule.

Wherever you are in this process, remember to write it down in your journal, put it in your planner, and schedule a time to review your goals. By setting clear priorities for yourself and committing to a schedule, your video creation plan is sure to succeed.

TIP 90: HELP! PRIORITIES ARE HARD

◀◀ ❙ ▶▶

Don't worry if, after reading the prior tips, you find yourself feeling overwhelmed and without any clear priorities for your videos. Some of us, for a variety of reasons, can struggle with priorities. If you feel stuck in that area, don't worry about it. I'm going to give you a few suggestions here for potential priorities that have worked for me. In other words, you can borrow my priorities to help you get started. After you have gotten into the work, I expect that your own priorities will bubble up.

One place where I've discovered helpful information for my videos is in my course evaluations. I know that student evaluations are problematic, but

I have found that they can be useful in certain circumstances. Take a look at some of your recent evaluations and notice if students referenced any particular assignments. Could you use this information to create a video tutorial about one of those assignments, increasing clarity and decreasing confusion?

Here's another approach: What is the most common question that you get from students each semester? Let's say that it's about your late policy. Some of you might have your own late policies, some might not have one at all, and others are using an institutional late policy. Whichever of those is true, I'm willing to bet that this is a common question. Frequently asked questions are an excellent topic for videos. In this case, you could make a short video explaining the logistics of the late policy and the reasons behind it.

Finally, perhaps you are reading this book because you are looking to get a boost at work to set yourself up for getting a promotion or tenure. There's nothing wrong with being motivated by external circumstances. Chat with your team about institutional priorities. For example, many institutions are focusing on diversity and equity. If that's the case, and you want to show that you are supporting that important initiative in your work, create a video sharing that value with your students.

Mining student evaluations, considering frequently asked questions, and identifying institutional goals are all sources of inspiration for your videos. If no clear priority appeared for you when you brainstormed, or you're having a tough time deciding, don't let that initial confusion stand in the way of your progress. Pick one of these suggestions and just get started. More information will come to you once you start doing the fun and intellectually stimulating work of creating videos.

TIP 91: WHEN IN DOUBT, CREATE A WELCOME VIDEO

◀◀ I ▶▶

You've read this book, you've brainstormed, and you've tried all my suggestions about developing priorities (or you've borrowed my example priorities). If you still feel stuck, this tip is a sort of "Video 9-1-1." I want everyone to leave this book having created at least one video.

If you're not sure where to start, let's keep it as simple as simple can be: Create a welcome video for your students. If everyone who reads this book does at least this, I'll be a very happy teacher. Welcome videos were the first type of videos that I created when I started teaching online. I continue to use them in every class that I teach.

Most of us know that the first few weeks of the college experience are a critical time for student success. Many institutions now front-load support resources into a structured first-year experience program to help get students off to a successful start. Whether you are teaching first-term students or not, I would imagine that you recognize the importance of the first week of your course. That's when we build connections with our students, establish expectations for each other, and clarify group norms.

In an online course, a welcome video can go a long way to setting the tone for the term. In flipped classes, a welcome video can be an additional layer of connection. The word *welcome* has very powerful connotations in this context. When we welcome our students to our courses, we let them know that we're glad they are enrolled. For many students, particularly first-generation students, this is a powerful message.

What should you include in a welcome video? Start by introducing yourself and give students a few telling details. These don't have to be personal; you could share your favorite food and the last book that you read. Then, introduce your course and tell students why this course will benefit them. Maybe it will help them become better thinkers or serve their communities. Other courses might offer very specific skills, such as knowledge of a computer software program. Help students see the relevance of your course. Finally, end with a few encouraging words, perhaps letting students know how they can reach you if they need assistance.

My welcome videos are usually about five minutes long, and I do a simple, headshot-type video. If that's not your preference, do a screencast with audio instead (see tip 76) or an animated video (see tip 77). You might want to have the screencast contain a simple slide with a few pictures that relate to you or your course.

When in doubt, start with a welcome video. Seeing that you are a human being who cares about their success will grab your students' attention from day one. If you continue to create additional videos, that's great. If not, a welcome video alone will boost the value of any course.

Position your smartphone's camera over Figure 91.1 to view a video about this tip.

Figure 91.1. Video: *When in Doubt, Create a Welcome Video.*

Note. Retrieved from https://youtu.be/d7cfxExLcUU

TIP 92: FOCUS ON THE POSITIVES

◀◀ ❘ ▶▶

Another concept that I want to offer as you build your plan for your video creation practice is that rather than focusing on what's broken, it's sometimes more effective to build on our strengths. If your video priorities haven't yet crystallized, consider a shift into a more positive mind-set. This might help to clarify your next steps.

Many of us tend to focus on the negative. Rick Hanson (2013), author of *Hardwiring Happiness: The New Brain Science of Contentment, Calm, and Confidence*, explains this negative tendency in terms of evolutionary brain science. In short, focusing on the negative has been what's kept our species alive to this point. However, in the modern era, where we have mastered many of the elements that used to be threats to us, this negative focus has started to do more harm than good. Hanson argues that even though our brains are like Velcro for negativity and Teflon for positivity, we can begin to practice the opposite: We can intentionally cultivate a more positive outlook.

Who are you at your best as a teacher? Take a few minutes to reflect on that question. You might even want to write down your answers in your teaching journal and do a bit of freewriting here. Picture yourself on your best day. What are you doing? How do you communicate with your students? What types of teaching choices do you make on that best day?

With that positive vision in mind, consider how you can use videos to support the great work you are already doing. Let's say that building personal connections with students feels tough for you, but you do a good job of creating unique assignments that challenge your students. Start there. Introduce one of your assignments in a video.

Let's flip that equation. Your greatest gift as a teacher is in the personal relationships that you build with your students. You have a fun sense of humor, and you feel at your best as a teacher when you're able to weave that humor into your course's content. Start there. Create a video with a funny story about your subject.

When we focus on the positive, it's often a lot easier to stay motivated when trying something new. This strengths-based approach can be used to help set your video priorities. Match your priorities with your teaching strengths to create your unique video creation practice.

Reference

Hanson, R. (2013). *Hardwiring happiness: The new brain science of contentment, calm, and confidence.* New York, NY: Harmony Books.

TIP 93: SEEK SUPPORT

◀◀ ❘ ▶▶

We are social animals, hardwired for connection (Lieberman, 2013). As an introvert, it took me a long time to admit to this reality, but it's certainly proven true in my life. While I like to pretend that I can go it alone, I need people. We all do. To develop your ideal video creation practice, it's important to seek support.

A good place to start is to consider which stakeholders on your campus might be invested in your video creation plan. Some likely candidates include the following departments: online learning, the teaching and learning center, technology, and disability services. It's worth sending an e-mail to your peers in each of these areas, letting them know you'd like to start adding videos to your courses and asking for their input.

In addition to a wealth of resources, you might find that institutional norms about how videos should be created and shared differ from your plan. Take time to investigate these norms and have open discussions about how you want to use videos. Some institutions, for example, might fall prey to the idea that all videos must be hyperproduced. Be prepared to explain the concept of humanizing online learning and the value of simple and sustainable videos.

I expect that we have reached a point in the education industry's trajectory where your plan will be met with open arms. However, if you do encounter resistance, be prepared to make a case for why you want to use videos in your courses. Share the research from this book that points to the potential benefits for both students and faculty.

Finally, your peers, both locally and globally, are a potential source of support. Much of what I learned about creating videos came from a combination of trial and error along with invaluable peer support. Colleagues would stop by my office and mention new video software that they were trying out. Online, via social media, I am continually learning about how to improve my videos and getting new ideas. Our fellow teachers and faculty are probably our most valuable resource.

I've learned that the amount of support that I receive is related to my willingness to share with others. The more that I share my work and have the courage to put myself out there, the more I gain in return. Start sharing, whether in person or online, the gifts and challenges of your video creation process, and you'll assuredly receive an equal measure of support in return.

Reference

Lieberman, M. D. (2013). *Social: Why our brains are wired to connect.* New York, NY: Broadway Books.

SECTION TWELVE

PRACTICE EXERCISES

I wouldn't be much of a teacher if I didn't help you practice the skills that you've just learned, would I? Practice is a chance to apply the principle of depth of processing, which will solidify these concepts in your brain and help them stick. The practice exercises that I've included in this section will also help you step outside of your comfort zone a bit. Some of them are silly, others more serious and heartfelt. If one of those types of exercises feels uncomfortable for you, guess what? That's probably the one that will benefit you the most.

You can certainly pick and choose from among these exercises, but I've been intentional about all of them, and you'll get the most bang for your buck by running through them all. They're all short, less than 5 minutes each, so in total, this section will take you about 30 minutes to complete. Thirty minutes to activate your creative muscles and enliven your videos seems like a worthy investment to me.

If even the titles of the practice exercises have you shaking your head, let me be clear that you don't have to share these with anyone. After you record a video and watch it back, delete it. No one ever needs to see these but you. Of course, if I open my e-mail tomorrow to find videos of your practice exercises, I'll be a very happy teacher. The choice is yours, and the most important thing is that you start to get comfortable exploring your on-screen energy.

After completing these exercises, you have reached the end of this book. You'll be ready to start creating awesome instructional videos for you and your students. Until then, it's time to practice.

TIP 94: IT'S STORYTIME

◀◀ ❙ ▶▶

Pull out a pen and piece of paper and jot down a list of some of your favorite stories in your teaching journal. These don't have to have anything to do with education because you're just practicing here. Focus on stories that have a clear narrative structure with a beginning, a middle, and an end. Once you have a solid list prepared, scan through it, and look for stories that you think you can tell in less than five minutes. Circle those stories and then pick the one that feels most comfortable and familiar.

Next, select your method of recording: computer webcam or smartphone. Don't overthink which of those options is the ideal fit. The goal in these practice exercises is discovery. In many ways, you can learn as much by making "bad" choices as you can from ideal decisions. If you spontaneously choose to record on your phone and realize that the camera was shaky the entire time, that's great information to discover. Now, record your video and tell your story.

After recording, watch your video and consider the following reflection questions. You might wish to write your answers in your teaching journal.

- Did you develop a sense of suspense and climax? How so? A good story starts slow and then builds.
- Did you vary your voice tone and body language to support the narrative arc, or did your voice and body language remain still and flat for most of the video?
- If this video found an audience, what would be the one-sentence takeaway from your story?
- List one to three positives that you noticed in your video. What did you do well?
- List one to three areas of opportunity for future improvement.

TIP 95: SAY A TONGUE TWISTER

◀◀ ❙ ▶▶

There is a great paradox of video creation for you to explore in this practice exercise. We want to speak clearly in our videos. The term for this is *elocution*. At the same time, it's okay to make mistakes. If you stumble over words once in a while, keep going. We are human beings, not robots. Finding a balance between those ideals will be part of your video creation journey. There are times when I twist my words, and I decide to restart my recordings after too many mistakes. However, in most cases, I correct myself and continue recording. This exercise will help you explore this balance.

Find a tongue twister (e.g., Sally saw 17 slippery snakes) either through an Internet search or, if you have little kids, their books. Don't go too easy on yourself here; you want to pick something that will challenge you and your elocution skills. Print or write it down so that you can reference it as you record or simply memorize it.

Start recording on your computer's webcam or smartphone. All you need to do in this video is to repeat the tongue twister 5 to 10 times. Make sure that you say it enough times so that your tongue is actually twisted; making mistakes is the goal here. Once you reach the point where you flub your words, keep going. This is the magic moment. Take a breath and try again. Can you slow down a bit, focus, and speak a clean version of the tongue twister after you've made a mistake, all while recording yourself on camera?

After recording and watching your video, consider the following reflection questions:

- What was your comfort level during this video? How did you feel while recording?
- Were you able to recover after making a mistake? What strategies did you use to recover?
- What is your normal speaking speed? Does this feel too slow, too fast, or just right for the videos that you want to create?
- How would you rate your elocution?
- Envision your ideal voice tone and speaking speed. Picture your best self. What do they look and sound like? Take a breath, close your eyes, and try to hear that voice in your head.

TIP 96: MAKE A MISTAKE

◄◄ ❙ ►►

In the last practice exercise, you created a video of yourself saying a tongue twister, which allowed you the chance to stumble over your words, right the ship, and continue forward. This video will be similar, but I want you to make a mistake while speaking about your current field of interest. There are a couple of reasons that we're going to explore these different types of mistakes.

Mistakes are wonderful. Someone told me recently that the purpose of making mistakes is to learn how to make more. Mistakes are an antidote to the devil of perfectionism, a disease that plagues many of us but that seems particularly rampant in higher education.

If the idea of intentional mistakes has you feeling uncomfortable, I encourage you to check out the work of Brené Brown, an academic and a writer who studies courage and vulnerability. She has reams of data on the value of breaking the habit of perfectionism and embracing vulnerability, and how that can help us live happier and healthier lives (Brown, 2012). The beauty of Brown's work is that she speaks from the heart, but she's also got tons of data.

Back to our mistake making. For some of us who are less comfortable making mistakes, we might have felt okay about doing this work in the context of a tongue twister. "Big deal. I made a mistake saying a kiddie rhyme." The idea of making a mistake when discussing your field of expertise might push other buttons, which is why you're going to practice that skill.

Yes, making a mistake in your videos and learning how to keep going is a skill. The goal in these videos is not to polish ourselves into some idealized version of what a professor should be. The goal is to be human. That's what will connect with our students, winning both their hearts and minds.

For this video, record yourself explaining some fundamental tenet in your field for about three to five minutes. As an example, I might choose to record myself discussing brain-based teaching or the simple and sustainable system of video creation. What is your most significant professional expertise?

Start recording and start talking. Since you're doing this off the cuff and without a script, the odds are that you're going to make a speaking mistake without any additional effort. If so, congrats! You're an expert mistake maker. If you've been speaking for a couple of minutes without any stumbles, flub on purpose. Go ahead. Use the wrong word for a major theory in your field or twist your words. Go blank and squeak out a few "Umms" in a row.

Then, just as we did in the prior practice exercise, take a breath, correct yourself, and keep going. Finish the video.

After recording and watching your video, consider the following reflection questions:

- How did it feel to make a mistake when discussing your area of expertise?
- Was this a different feeling than you experienced during the tongue twister exercise?
- Are you open to the idea of making a few mistakes in your videos? Can you see how that could benefit you and your students?
- How will you determine whether to keep recording or restart after making a mistake?

Reference

Brown, B. (2012). *Daring greatly: How the courage to be vulnerable transforms the way we live, love, parent, and lead.* New York, NY: Avery.

TIP 97: TELL A JOKE

◀◀ I ▶▶

When I was fresh out of college, I was preparing for one of my first job interviews. I did an online search for common interview questions and came upon a list that included this prompt: Tell us a joke. I can remember being overcome by a sense of horror. If that comes up in an interview, I thought, I will either faint or throw up on the spot. Years later, when I was teaching college and career success strategies to first-year college students, I always told them that story and used that as an example of being prepared for the unexpected in job interviews.

There's a certain pressure to telling a good joke because it's not just about remembering the content; it's also about timing and delivery. That's why you're going to use this practice exercise to become more comfortable on camera. As the saying goes, the only way out is through. To get to comfort, we have to traverse discomfort.

To begin, think of a joke. Ideally, your joke will be a bit complex with a short introduction followed by a punch line. If you choose to go with a good ol' knock-knock joke, you might find value in telling a few of those in your video. If you don't know any jokes, ask a friend.

Once you have your joke or jokes prepared, start recording. Aim to be on camera for at least a minute.

After recording and watching your video, consider the following reflection questions:

- How did you feel while recording the video? Compare your comfort level to how you felt during the previous practice exercises.
- When watching your video, notice your voice tone, facial expressions, and body language. How did those change when you told your punch line?
- What strategies can you take from this exercise and apply to your instructional videos? What did you learn about your presentation skills and delivery?

TIP 98: MAKE MUSIC WITH YOUR VOICE

◀◀ I ▶▶

I played the violin throughout middle and high school as a member of my school's orchestra. It's been a long time since I played, but I still remember some of the musical notations. *Piano* meant to play very softly. *Forte* meant to get loud. Within any piece of music, we'd follow those notations, sometimes starting very quietly and then building to a thunderous conclusion. Other times, we'd shift back and forth from piano to forte, then back again, keeping our audience on their toes (or ears, I suppose). These changes conveyed different energies based on what the composer wanted listeners to feel.

For this practice exercise, record a video of yourself speaking and varying the volume of your voice. Start very quietly. As you continue talking, begin to get louder, and louder, and louder, until at the end of your video, you are practically yelling. Then, for your final few sentences, drop back to piano, speaking in a whisper. In terms of content, you can choose to talk about anything in this video. You could even read from a document if you prefer. The goal of this video is not to focus on the content but your voice.

After recording and watching your video, consider the following reflection questions:

- How did the piano, or quiet voice tone, feel for you? What does a softer sound convey to your audience?
- How did the forte, or loud voice tone, feel for you? What does a loud voice convey to your audience?
- Notice the shift from soft to loud and back again. Does that shift capture attention?
- How can you vary your voice tone to keep your videos compelling and to capture your students' attention? How can different voice tones help convey information in videos?

TIP 99: SPEAK FROM YOUR HEART

◀◀ I ▶▶

I've saved what might be the toughest exercise for many of you for last. Your mission is simple but not easy. Start recording, and then speak from your heart. If that's enough direction for you, skip the next paragraph and get to work.

If you're looking for some additional ideas to get you started here, record a video where you speak to the person you love most in the world, telling them how you feel about them. You could also record something of a "last lecture." If you knew that today was your last day on Earth, what knowledge would you want to leave behind? Talk about something that you love or the last time that you felt overwhelmed with love for someone or something. What has been the greatest challenge in your life thus far? The key here is to connect your words with your heart.

Record this video, where you'll speak from the heart. Aim for at least a couple of minutes of content.

After recording and watching your video, consider the following reflection questions:

- How did it feel to focus on speaking from the heart rather than a more logical or intellectual approach?
- Compare this video to the previous videos. How did your tone or presentation differ? Was your body language or voice different? How so?
- Consider how you can adapt this work to your instructional videos. How can you remain professional and appropriate while also speaking from your heart?

Position your smartphone's camera over Figure 99.1 to view a video about this tip.

Figure 99.1. Video: *Speak From Your Heart.*

Note. Retrieved from https://youtu.be/-WGVWtJixik

CONCLUSION

I have found that writing about something helps me know what I really think and feel about it. Writing has given me this gift time and again, but I didn't see it coming in my writing about videos. I've been so close to videos for so long (since high school) that I didn't think I'd uncover any new terrain. And yet, my thoughts and feelings about videos, online education, and teaching were further clarified by the experience of writing this book.

The more I wrote, the more it became clear that this book isn't just about how to make videos using a simple and sustainable system. Rather, it's about the chance for faculty to practice creativity in their work, about the singular importance of the student–teacher relationship, and about the type of educational models that educators will create in the years to come. My hope, therefore, is that you have not only created some great videos to share with your students but also gained some inspiration for your teaching journey as a whole.

Educators: Thank you for all that you do. It is difficult. It is seen. It is invaluable.

ABOUT THE AUTHOR

Karen Costa is a career higher education professional with a passion for supporting students and faculty, particularly in the online learning environment. Her work is centered around teaching college success strategies to first-year students, online pedagogy, and faculty development.

Costa is a staff writer for *Women in Higher Education*. Her writing has also appeared in *Inside Higher Ed. The Philadelphia Inquirer, On Being*, and *Faculty Focus*. She is involved in various faculty development initiatives including as a facilitator for Faculty Guild.

Costa graduated with honors from Syracuse University with a BA in sociology. She holds an MEd in higher education from the University of Massachusetts Amherst and a CAGS in educational leadership from Northeastern University. A proud lifelong learner, Costa recently received a professional certification in trauma and resilience from Florida State University and will complete her certificate in neuroscience, learning, and online instruction from Drexel University in early 2020. Costa is a certified yoga teacher and Level 1 Yoga for Arthritis teacher. She lives in Massachusetts with her family.

Connect with Karen Costa at http://www.karencostawriter.com or on Twitter @KarenRayCosta.

REFERENCES

Aubrey, K., & Riley, A. (2016). *Understanding and using educational theories.* Los Angeles, CA: SAGE.

Athabasca University. (n.d.). *The community of inquiry.* Retrieved from http://bb coi.athabascau.ca

Brown, B. (2012). *Daring greatly: How the courage to be vulnerable transforms the way we live, love, parent, and lead.* New York, NY: Avery.

Bubbl. (n.d.) *Home.* Retrieved from https://bubbl.us/

California State University. (n.d.). *Behaviors and strategies for improving online instructor presence.* Retrieved from http://page.teachingwithoutwalls.com/instructorpresencestrategiesci

CAST. (n.d.) *The UDL guidelines.* Retrieved from http://udlguidelines.cast.org/

Cavanagh, S. R. (2016). *The spark of learning: Energizing the college classroom with the science of emotion.* Morgantown: West Virginia University Press.

Cavanagh, S. R. (2019, May 16). Investigating emotion-based interventions in the college classroom: Mindfulness and cognitive reappraisal. *Invitation to Learning: Emotions, Inclusivity, and Community.* Conference conducted at Assumption College, Worcester, Massachusetts.

Cox, R. (2009). *The college fear factor.* Cambridge, MA: Harvard University Press.

Coyle, D. (2009). *The talent code: Greatness isn't born. It's grown. Here's how.* New York, NY: Bantam.

Damasio, A. (1994). *Descartes' error: Emotion, reason, and the human brain.* New York, NY: Putnam.

Dixson, M. D. (2010). Creating effective student engagement in online courses: What do students find engaging? *Journal of Scholarship of Teaching and Learning, 10*(2), 1–13.

Draus, P. J., Curran, M. J., & Trempus, M. S. (2014). The influence of instructor-generated video content on student satisfaction with and engagement in asynchronous online classes. MERLOT *Journal of Online Teaching and Learning, 10*(2), 240–254.

Edwards, M. (2016, May 30). *YogAlign: Change your posture, change your life.* Workshop presented at Kripalu Yoga Centre, Stockbridge, MA.

Garrison, D. R., Anderson, T., & Archer, W. (2000). Critical inquiry in a text-based environment: Computer conferencing in higher education. *The Internet and Higher Education, 2*(2–3), 87–105.

Gehlbach, H., Brinkworth, M. E., King, A. M., Hsu, L. M., McIntyre, J., & Rogers, T. (2016). Creating birds of similar feathers: Leveraging similarity to improve teacher–student relationships and academic achievement. *Journal of Educational Psychology, 108*(3), 342–352.

Hanson, R. (2013). *Hardwiring happiness: The new brain science of contentment, calm, and confidence.* New York, NY: Harmony Books.

Hardiman, M. (2012). *The brain-targeted teaching model for 21st century schools.* Thousand Oaks, CA: SAGE.

Horvath, J. C. (2014). The neuroscience of PowerPoint™. *Mind, Brain, and Education, 8*(3), 137–142.

Isaacs, S. (2015). The difference between gamification and game-based learning. *ASCD Inservice.* Retrieved from http://inservice.ascd.org/the-difference-between-gamification-and-game-based-learning/

Jaggars, S. S., & Xu, D. (2016). How do online course design features influence student performance? *Computers & Education, 95*, 270–284.

Jensen, E. (2005). *Teaching with the brain in mind.* Alexandria, VA: ASCD.

Jones, S. J., & Long, V. M. (2013). Learning equity between online and on-site mathematics courses. *MERLOT Journal of Online Learning and Teaching, 9*(1), 1–12.

Lidwell, W., Holden, K., & Butler, J. (2003). *Universal principles of design: 125 ways to enhance usability, influence perception, increase appeal, make better design decisions, and teach through design.* Beverly, MA: Rockport Publishers.

Lieberman, M. D. (2013). *Social: Why our brains are wired to connect.* New York, NY: Broadway Books.

Loch, B., Jordan, C., Lowe, T., & Mestel, B. (2014). Do screencasts help to revise prerequisite mathematics? An investigation of student performance and perception. *International Journal of Mathematics Education, 45*(2), 256–268.

Mager, R. F. (1968). *Developing attitude toward learning.* Palo Alto, CA: Fearon Publishers.

Martin, F., Budhrani, K., Kumar, S., & Ritzhaupt, A. (2019). Award-winning faculty online teaching practices: Roles and competencies. *Online Learning Journal, 23*(1), 184–205.

Martin, F., Wang, C., & Sadaf, A. (2018). Student perception of helpfulness of facilitation strategies that enhance instructor presence, connectedness, engagement, and learning in online courses. *The Internet and Higher Education, 37*, 52–65.

Medina, J. (2008). *Brain rules: 12 principles for surviving and thriving at work, home, and school.* Seattle, WA: Pear Press.

Moore, M. (1997). Theory of transactional distance. In D. Keegan (Ed.), *Theoretical principles of distance education* (pp. 22–38). New York, NY: Routledge. Retrieved from http://www.c3l.uni-oldenburg.de/cde/found/moore93.pdf

Morpheus [Digital image]. (n.d.). Retrieved from https://imgflip.com/i/46zvm

Morris, C., & Chikwa, G. (2013). Screencasts: How effective are they and how do students engage with them? *Active Learning in Higher Education, 15*(1), 25–37.

Pacansky-Brock, M. (n.d.) How to humanize your online class. Retrieved from https://www.brocansky.com/humanizing-infographic

Penman, M. (2015, October 13). *In the classroom, common ground can transform GPAs* [Audio podcast]. Retrieved from https://www.npr.org/2015/10/13/444446708/in-the-classroom-common-ground-can-transform-gpas

Pryal, K. R. G. (2017). *Life of the mind interrupted: Essays on mental health and disability in higher education.* Chapel Hill, NC: Snowraven Books.

Quotes.com. (n.d.). *Thomas Carruthers.* Retrieved from https://www.quotes.net/quote/11642

Radicioni, B. (2018). *New study: Distance education up, overall enrollments down.* Retrieved from https://www.babson.edu/about/news-events/babson-announcements/babson-survey-research-group-tracking-distance-education-report/

Rendon, L. (1994). Validating culturally diverse students: Toward a new model of learning and student development. *Innovative Higher Education, 19*(1), 33–51. Retrieved from https://www.csuchico.edu/ourdemocracy/_assets/documents/pedagogy/rendon,-l.-1994---validation-theory.pdf

Reynolds, G. (2012). *Presentation Zen: Simple ideas on presentation design and delivery.* Berkeley, CA: New Riders.

Russell, T. (2001). *The nosignificant difference phenomenon: A comparative research annotated bibliography on technology for distance education.* Chicago, IL: IDECC.

Simon, H. A. (1956). Rational choice and the structure of the environment. *Psychological Review, 63*(2), 129–138.

Shyamalan, M.K. (1999). *The Sixth Sense.* Retrieved from http://www.lexwilliford.com/Workshops/Screenwriting/Scripts/Adobe%20Acrobat%20Scripts/Sixth%20Sense.pdf

Talking Heads. (1983). Burning down the house. On *Speaking in tongues* [album]. Sire.

Terada, Y. (2018). Welcoming students with a smile. *Edutopia.* Retrieved from https://www.edutopia.org/article/welcoming-students-smile

Tinto, V. (1993). *Leaving college: Rethinking the causes and cures of student attrition.* Chicago, IL: University of Chicago Press.

Torres, N. (2015, September). Gazing at nature makes you more productive: An interview with Kate Lee. *Harvard Business Review.* Retrieved from https://hbr.org/2015/09/gazing-at-nature-makes-you-more-productive

Tucker, B. (2012, Winter). The flipped classroom. *Education Next.* Retrieved from https://www.educationnext.org/the-flipped-classroom/

Weinstein, Y., & Smith, M. (2016). Learn how to study using . . . spaced practice. *The Learning Scientists.* Retrieved from http://www.learningscientists.org/blog/2016/7/21-1

Whitman, G., & Kelleher, I. (2016). *Neuroteach: Brain science and the future of education.* Lanham, MD: Rowman & Littlefield.

Wolitzer, M. (2008). *The ten-year nap.* New York, NY: Penguin.

Xu, D., & Jaggars, S. S. (2013). Adaptability to online learning: Differences across types of students and academic subject areas. *Community College Research Center, 54,* 1–32. Retrieved from https://ccrc.tc.columbia.edu/media/k2/attachments/adaptability-to-online-learning.pdf

Zak, P. (2015, February 2). Why inspiring stories make us react: The neuroscience of narrative. *Cerebrum,* Jan–Feb. Retrieved from https://www.ncbi.nlm.nih.gov/pmc/articles/PMC4445577/

INDEX

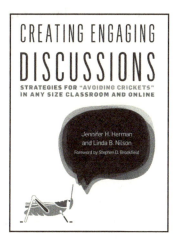

Creating Engaging Discussions

Strategies for "Avoiding Crickets" in Any Size Classroom and Online

Jennifer H. Herman and Linda B. Nilson

Foreword by Stephen D. Brookfield

"I've stolen a lot from this book. I regard myself as an avid collector of new pedagogic baubles and love it when I stumble across a new way to engage my students as I have done many times by reading Herman and Nilson's work. I have no doubt that as you read this book your own collection of discussion-based teaching strategies will be significantly enlarged."—**Stephen D. Brookfield**, *University of St. Thomas, Minneapolis-St. Paul*

Sty/us

22883 Quicksilver Drive
Sterling, VA 20166-2019   Subscribe to our e-mail alerts: www.Styluspub.com

Jump-Start Your Online Classroom

Mastering Five Challenges in Five Days

David S. Stein and Constance E. Wanstreet

"The brevity of *Jump-Start Your Online Classroom* should not be underestimated. Based on practical application of the content and concepts, its organization contains helpful hints on various aspects of successfully constructing a learner-centered, virtual classroom experience. The organization of the book is its greatest strength. Its five-day approach is based on the following challenges: (a) making the transition to online teaching, (b) building online spaces for learning, (c) preparing students for online learning, (d) managing and facilitating the online classroom, and (e) assessing learner outcomes. Although this book is marketed toward the novice online instructor, its approach, organization, and content make it a foundational tool that could have long-term value in troubleshooting and future course design."—***Reflective Teaching***

(Continues on preceding page)

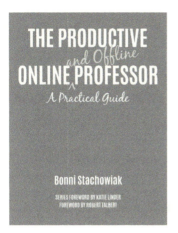

The Productive Online and Offline Professor

A Practical Guide

Bonni Stachowiak

Series Foreword by Kathryn E. Linder

Foreword by Robert Talbert

The Productive Online and Offline Professor is a practical guide for how to provide high-quality online classes to diverse students. This book shares specific technology and other tools that may be used in charting a course toward greater productivity. It is intended to be a professional resource for fulfilling our roles with excellence and joy while managing other priorities in our personal and professional lives.

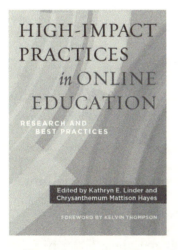

High-Impact Practices in Online Education

Research and Best Practices

Edited by Kathryn E. Linder and Chrysanthemum Mattison Hayes

Foreword by Kelvin Thompson

"*High-Impact Practices in Online Education* asks the right questions about online teaching and learning. This collection offers grounded, practical suggestions for evolving online pedagogy toward a purposeful form of teaching that offers possibilities beyond anything we've done until now."—**Matthew Reed**, *Vice President for Learning-Brookdale Community College*

(Continues on preceding page)

Also available from Stylus

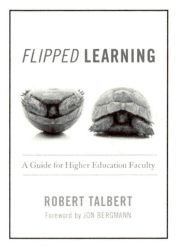

Flipped Learning

A Guide for Higher Education Faculty

Robert Talbert

Foreword by Jon Bergmann

"Robert Talbert provides the ultimate guide to flipping the classroom—moving the information transfer out of the classroom and the thinking back in! Whether you are considering revising your approach to teaching or you are already a seasoned 'flipper,' this book is a must-have reference."
—**Eric Mazur**, *Harvard University*

"The course design process, the tools and tips, and the excellent index make *Flipped Learning* worth a read."—***Technical Communications***

Thrive Online

A New Approach to Building Expertise and Confidence as an Online Educator

Shannon Riggs

Series Foreword by Kathryn E. Linder

Foreword by Penny Ralston-Berg

"There is truly something for everyone in *Thrive Online*, including faculty preparing to teach their first online course, experienced online faculty, busy administrators, and online leaders making policy decisions. Readers are encouraged to deeply interact with the material through timely best practices, practical pointers and actionable checklists, thoughtful reflection questions, and a compelling invitation to connect with others in the #ThriveOnline community."—**Tina Parscal**, *Executive Director of CCCOnline, Colorado Community College System*

(Continues on preceding page)